Thirty Days of Thankfulness

Finding Reasons to Be Thankful In Everyday Life

April J. Durham

ISBN: 1499597754
ISBN-13: 978-1499597752

Dedication

To Patrick, Diddle, and Hubby, for sharing this beautiful walk with me and making my life complete—I love you!

To Mom and Daddy, for believing in me and never giving up on me. Thanks, too, for supporting my dreams and giving me the best gift any person could ask for—my faith in Jesus.

To my Aunt Kelly, for being my best friend, my ear to listen, and my shoulder to cry on—I am thankful for you

To all the amazing, supportive people who encouraged me along the way as I worked on this book and my thankful journey

~~~

A Very Special Thanks

Special thanks to Karie Cromer King for saying you loved to read my writing. Those are the words every writer longs to hear. Your continual support and the kind words you said about my writing so many times made me feel like you were my personal cheering section. I couldn't have done it without you. Thanks!

Special thanks to Kathy Hayes for telling me how you looked forward to reading my thankful posts every evening after work. Those, too, are words that every writer dreams to hear. You gave me hope that I might actually make it as an author. Thanks!

Special thanks to Amanda Ellis Watkins for sharing one of my thankful stories with others and encouraging me. You gave me hope that my words were worth sharing. Thanks!

Ladies, so many days your words kept me going, and I could not be more grateful for your encouragement. Today I am thankful for each of you. THANK YOU!
~~~

"Always give thanks for everything to our God and Father in the name of our Lord Jesus Christ."

Ephesians 5:20, *The Living Bible*

Contents

Introduction	vii
Prologue	ix
Day 1: A 1960s Lite Brite	1
Day 2: Popsicles	4
Day 3: Plastic pumpkins	7
Day 4: A Hand-Me-Down Sewing Machine	11
Day 5: Pancakes	15
Day 6: A DVD Player	19
Day 7: Bench Swings.	24
Day 8: A Yard Full of Dead Leaves	28
Day 9: A Southern Accent	32
Day 10: Ladybugs	36
Day 11: Miracles	40
Day 12: Time	46
Day 13: Blankets	49
Day 14: Books	52
Day 15: Dogs	55
Day 16: Index Cards	59
Day 17: Tape	62
Day 18: Liquid Soap	65
Day 19: Forgiveness	68
Day 20: Commas	71
Day 21: Rainy Days	75
Day 22: Deadlines.	78
Day 23: Pipe Tobacco	81
Day 24: To Have a King	84
Day 25: Technology	88
Day 26: Ties	91
Day 27: Creditors	94
Day 28: Groceries	97
Day 29: Crayons	100
Day 30: Second Chances	103
Epilogue	107
About the Author	108

"Oh, give thanks to the Lord, for he is good
His love and his kindness go on forever."
1 Chronicles 16:34. *The Living Bible*

Introduction

I started writing this book on October 31, 2013. That first day, I began simply with the prologue, plotting out my journey and explaining to all of my friends and family I connect with on social media sites my goal for November to write thirty essays about thankfulness. As a result, the book you are now holding turned out much like a personal journey. At the end, I issued a challenge to you, the reader, to take your own thirty-day thankfulness challenge. I even encouraged you to start that very day.

As I got ready to put the book to press, however, I decided that the best way to get others to take the challenge would be to ask them to take it with me. For that reason, I have included in this book pages where you can actually write down your thankful thoughts every day for thirty days. They don't have to be essays. They don't even have to be complete sentences! Whatever you happen to feel thankful for that day will do just fine, but I do encourage you to stick with it and strive to be thankful for the next thirty days. Then, at the end of thirty days, I have another challenge for you instead.

Hopefully, this book will be an enjoyable read for you, and, hopefully, you will enjoy the thirty-day thankfulness challenge. It truly changed my life, so I know firsthand that it can make a difference. I pray that it will make a difference for you as well.

Best wishes and happy reading!

"No wonder I give thanks to you, O Lord, among the nations, and sing praises to your name."
2 Samuel 22:50, *The Living Bible*

Prologue

In 2012, I ran across an interesting post by a friend on Facebook saying that she was going to begin a thirty-day challenge to find things to be thankful for and share them with her friends and family. I decided it sounded like a great idea, so I joined her and dozens of other friends as we began to post about the things we were thankful for in our lives. I started with the essentials: my children, my husband, the Lord. I was thankful for a home, a car, and things I am consciously thankful for most every day. As the month wore on, the thankfulness kept coming, but some days it was harder to find than others. The thing that held me up was that I was being thankful for the things I was usually thankful for, and that list was used up pretty quickly. In fact, I ran it down in short form daily in blessings for meals and prayers with the children. I never stopped to think if I was truly appreciative or not. I knew I was supposed to be. I said I was. Yet, somehow, the more I wrote, the more I wondered if I really meant what I was saying. Not that I didn't feel thankful for things like a car, a house, and family or friends. I did. I just felt something was missing in my thankful journey.

I noticed, too, that as the month went by, fewer and fewer of my friends continued to post their thankful thoughts. I started to think maybe I was not alone in my battle to find thankfulness. Maybe the world was too big and crazy to have a thirty-day supply of gratitude. Maybe we all had said the same things and couldn't think of anything new. Or maybe we just let the world win, sucking us back into the daily grind, far from thinking outside our daily thankful box.

Looking back over the first ten days of the month, my posts had been "Liked" by fifteen or more friends. People commented and chimed in. Other friends had posted their thankfulness in abundance, some racing to catch up in the thankfulness race because it felt so good to join in. I was no exception. I was a day late getting started and posted my first thankful post right before my second. What had seemed so inviting and heart-warming those first few days seemed to have changed as the month grew longer. By the fifteenth day, few friends were still posting thankful posts, and those that did rarely posted more than a few words. And the "Likes" and comments on my own posts about thankfulness were completely absent on some days. I knew not everyone was as long-winded as I was, nor liked to read as much as I wrote, but the feeling just changed. It seemed the challenge to share what I was thankful for each day for thirty days had indeed become challenging. Especially for me.

I tried to renew my vigor. I was a thankful person after all, and I wanted everyone to know I was thankful. I wanted them to feel thankful, too. Some days it worked. Some days I could muster the words to feel thankful myself and, on a rare occasion, inspire a comment or "Like" from my friends. By the end of the month, I was far more frustrated by my failure to feel thankful for finishing the challenge than I was excited on the first day I rushed to join in. I had done it. I mean, I had written the words day in and day out for thirty days. I had said my prayers to the Lord and told him of my thankfulness. Why, then, did I not feel better? Not feel more blessed?

I searched for that answer throughout December. I continued my search into January and even into February. It wasn't until one amazingly low day in February, hiding in the bathroom for some quiet time alone, crying out my eyes, praying to the Lord for guidance and a way out of my hopelessness, that I realized the problem. I wasn't really thankful at all. I thought I was. I wanted to be. But I wasn't. The Lord blessed me that day with His Grace and His Peace, and I saw for the first time in more years than I could count that I wasn't grateful for what I had. It had been so long since I was truly grateful that I couldn't remember what it actually felt like. Sure, I had felt obligated to be thankful. I had felt like I had to be grateful since the Lord had blessed me with more things than I could ever imagine. Yet, I failed to realize that anyone can be thankful for what is right in front of them. Even me. What I *needed* was to take the time to be thankful for the things that I didn't see laid out before me. Those things I took for granted every single day of my life.

I'm not saying that everyone I know or who has completed this thankfulness challenge is not thankful. In fact, I believe that everyone who tries it is grateful for the things they write about and talk about. If they weren't, then why would they take the time to share them? Being thankful has to come from something good inside us, and surely some good is shared from even trying. I think the world just takes over, and somehow it seems easier to get sucked back into the daily routine of life where thankfulness often takes a back seat.

So, this year, I am re-taking the challenge to be thankful each day for thirty days. I am stretching my mind and my heart and trying to find things I would not normally be thankful for along with the things I am thankful for every day. I am also adding my own challenge to it. My challenge is to take time each day to stop and read or listen to what someone else is thankful for in his or her life. And maybe—just maybe—I will come away from this year's challenge feeling a little more blessed, a lot less stressed, and with a whole new repertoire of things to be thankful for as each day passes. Hopefully after reading about my journey, you will, too.

Thanks for reading and God bless!

April J. Durham

Day 1: Today I am thankful for a 1960s Lite Brite.

As a child, I always wanted a Lite Brite, but I never actually owned one. I remember visiting friends and playing with those shiny little plastic pegs, taking care to insert each one into just the right letter of the black construction paper designs. The light shining through the beautiful colors made me think of the magic of Christmas at any time of the year. A couple weeks ago, we found an original 1960s Lite Brite in a thrift store for four dollars. The kids were so excited, I decided to take a chance. They used the last of their birthday money to buy it, hoping it would really work and hoping we could find template sheets to fit.

When we got home there was much anticipation as we opened up the tattered box. We prayed that the tiny tag put on by the thrift store reading "WORKS" was true and plugged it in. With a slight sizzle of frying dust and the pungent smell to match, the giant bulb inside glowed brighter than any of the compact fluorescents of our day could ever hope to reach. The kids laughed with glee. Hub reached into the box and pulled out a flat box full of black sheets covered in white letters. The excitement grew! Almost all of the sheets were unused! Diddle reached in and pulled out a small plastic container of plastic pegs. There were five more as well, each in their own re-used Ruth's Salads containers, brittle plastic browned with age, each displaying its original price tags in the 50-60 cents range. Everyone was ecstatic!

We placed the first black sheet on the peg board, and the children began to insert the pegs. There were no white pegs or yellow, and some colors had fewer than others, but it was so much fun! Peg by peg, the glow increased, and the picture of a Halloween witch took form. Her glowing green face and purple hair. Her orange broomstick and blue trails of movement behind. It was magic in the making. Nimble little fingers pushed and prodded each peg into place until all the letters were covered except for a few. Careful re-planning moved the orange from the broom to the moon since the orange pegs had run out quickly from covering for the lost whites and yellows. The violet broom still flew straight as the orange moon made a full crescent.

Finally, the work was done! Hub ran around the house turning out all the lights. That little witch soared in the black of the night! It was amazing, and the laughter that accompanied that first flight was beyond all compare. We giggled and gawked as that witch flew high on her electrically glowing pegs. Even Daddy had a good time watching the children crouch before the glowing scene to dream big dreams and imagine the worlds they could make from little plastic pegs and light behind black construction paper.

Since that wonderful first night, the children look forward to playing with their Lite Brite. Each evening, they sit before the little white triangular machine, pushing pegs into place and watching as new worlds glow into existence. And better still, the magic those twinkling little lights held for me as a child is now shared with two of the people I hold most dear on the earth, my children. Yes, today I am grateful for a used 1960s Lite Brite, and I hope to be thankful for it for many years to come.

Day 1: What are you thankful for today?

Day 2: Today I am thankful for popsicles.

As a child, I enjoyed popsicles as much as any other kid. On a hot, sunny day in the South, a popsicle ranked right up there with a brand new charm from the dime store for my charm necklace or a new Frisbee to replace one that got lost in the woods. Cold and refreshing, packed with sugar and dye, those frozen pieces of ice on a stick were a great treat. As I got older, however, my love of popsicles diminished. I didn't have much time or use for them, too busy to stop for something so simple. My tastes seemed to change, and I left those frozen pops alone for many years. Slowly, I began to be annoyed with the popsicle. Peeling off the waxed paper wrapper and rinsing off the ice crystals coating the treat just didn't have the charm it did as a child. I gave them up.

It wasn't until I was almost thirty that I rediscovered the popsicle. I got dysentery. Yes, the horrible disease people die of in third world countries. I got it from eating celery at work one night. Apparently it was going around in celery at the time, but I didn't know it. Believe me, I found out quickly. It was a horrible experience that had me down from Christmas to New Year's, and popsicles became my main food source. My taste for them began to renew itself. Cool and refreshing and with actual flavor. Yes, popsicles were my favorite food for over a week. I even discovered that when you ate the whole box in a week that the little ice crystals didn't form as much. Popsicles seemed to be on the way back up, but, of course, as soon as I was well they were quickly forgotten.

Time passed, and I once again found myself without really having much use for popsicles. The occasional stomach bug would coax me into buying a box, but, just as in years past, the frozen pops would sit in the freezer until they were one big block of ice, and I would toss them out. Pregnancy didn't even spark my taste for the frozen treats of childhood. I thought maybe I was done with the popsicle.

Then my son was born. My daughter Diddle was a year older then Hub, and, luckily, she was a pretty healthy child as far as colds and viruses went. Hub, however, was not so lucky. That poor child had a runny nose from the time he could sit up on his own. He had the sniffles for what felt like every day of his life, and even daily doses of Zyrtec didn't stop the runny nose until he was almost a year old. Once he was large enough for a bigger dose of medicine, his allergies got a little better. With the good comes the bad, I suppose, and Hub ended up with a persistent dry throat from the medicine. He was miserable, and no amount of drinking seemed to ease the uncomfortable feeling in his throat. We turned to the old reliable stand-by—the popsicle.

Popsicles were Hub's liberator from the cough and scratchiness of a constant dry throat. He loved them. As big and active as Hub was and as little junk food as he ate, the doctor and I had no problem adding the 35 calorie frozen treats to his daily intake. He would eat three or four a day. As he got used to eating them, he learned that they were a great way for his throat to feel better. We had almost given up hope that we would be able to get his thirst under control. Popsicles did the trick! Yes, popsicles, again, had saved the day.

As Hub has grown from allergy-stricken baby to allergy-ridden child, his love for popsicles has grown. With all the flavors and colors and styles available these days, we can buy a different kind each week. Sometimes two kinds a week. He walks around a good bit of the day with a popsicle in his hand. These days he gets his own popsicles, unwraps them, and even reads us all the jokes from the stick. They add a little bit of Hubby humor into our days and nights. Sure, he wears the popsicle-colored smile from time to time, but it suits him well. Hub is our happy little man, and popsicles helped make that so. They gave a thirsty child a way to feel relief, and they earned their way into being a permanent fixture in our family.

I have no doubts that one day in the not-so-distant future Hub may outgrow his love of popsicles. It is definitely possible. I did it myself. But, one thing is for sure: I am grateful for those little frozen pops and the reprieve they have given a little boy with such horrible allergies. Sure, I am grateful for the childhood memories and the helping hand through the worst Christmas-week stomach malady I have ever known. But it was this last feat that popsicles accomplished—making my child's life a little more comfortable—that has earned them their own shelf in my freezer. I am sure that the last box I own will probably be a frozen block like many of those I have thrown away in the past, but I have my doubts that I will ever see a day when they don't grace my home. I also know I will always be grateful for the miracle they performed in our lives.

Day 2: What are you thankful for today?

Day 3: Today I am thankful for plastic pumpkins.

Halloween has come and gone, but its vestiges remain. Of these, the dearest to my heart is the plastic pumpkin. You know the ones I'm talking about: the silly little orange ones with black triangle eyes and nose and sporting a crooked smile, their thin plastic sturdy yet flexible. Today these plastic candy holders appear in purple, pink, and green, and their eyes and mouth have more curve and softness than the triangles and jagged grins of yore. Still, the old-fashioned orange ones remain one of my favorite parts of fall.

As a child the re-appearance of those orange and black buckets meant Halloween was around the corner. For years, my brother and I carried the same plastic pumpkins, holding those thin black plastic handles until the weight of the candy inside etched a red line into the palm of our hands. As young children, those pumpkins meant not only candy but magic. You see, Halloween was the one night a year that I got a night off from the fight I have fought all of my life.

My brother David was born with more disabilities than most people know exist. He had cerebral palsy, epilepsy, severe brain damage, a tongue that was partially paralyzed, and more physical disabilities than I ever care to name. There were other disabilities with fancy names, but in the end we all described his condition as severely mentally retarded, a term that was used in those days regularly without any politically incorrect reservations. I came to hate that term *retarded.* Nearly every fight in my life has had something to do with that word. I hated that people thought *retarded* meant *stupid* because my brother was far from stupid. He was scary intelligent. He just didn't have the ability to relay his intelligence to the world. I hated that people used the word *retarded* as a derogatory term because, in my life, David was my closest friend and the most loving person I ever knew. And so, most of the time, I just hated the world.

Day in and day out, I fought what felt like the whole world and their misguided beliefs that they were normal and anyone who didn't look or act like them was wrong. I was born into this world with David already here. He was my very first friend and my first child as well. He took care of me, and I took care of him. Sure, we fought, but when you had so many barriers between you, it was hard not to have frustrations and flared tempers from time to time. The older we got, the more the fighting increased. Looking back, I realize that the older David got, the more frustrating the world got. As a child, it felt like the bigger the world got, the more David got left behind, and, thus, the harder I had to try to pull him along. It was a big job for a kid, but it was one I gladly bore. Still, the day-to-day weight of it was a lot for me.

There was, however, one night a year that I got to lay down that cross. A night that the world's boundaries faded and the invisible lines that surrounded those considered *in* and those considered *out* lost their power to restrain. And every year, the re-appearance of those orange, plastic pumpkins meant it was almost there. That one magical night when my brother who was so very different from everyone else finally got to be the person he really was, someone who wasn't that different after all. The night of Halloween.

As a child, we were lucky enough to get costumes with those silly plastic masks that we strapped on with a string of elastic. Today those hot, plastic smother-traps aren't used anymore. Air holes that were insufficient or something like that I'm sure was the cause. But back then, we thought they were the grandest thing ever. The first one I remember wearing went with a Wonder Woman costume that was at least three sizes too big for me. It had the gold crown and red diamond in the middle just like what I thought was the real thing. That year David got a Darth Vader mask. He would put it on and his regular heavy-breathing mimicked the enormous respirations of the villain of all villains as if on purpose. It was great!

And then it happened. Halloween came, and we got dressed up to go. We picked up our orange plastic pumpkins and headed out into the night on a grand adventure. Down came our masks, and the world faded away. We were no longer ourselves, or so it would seem to the outside world. To house after house we would trek, arms extended, plastic pumpkins dangling, and the candy rivers would flow. No one stared at us. No one shied away. No funny looks. No names being called. No nothing. And all we had to do was say the magic words and candy and praises were ours. Trick or treat! My brother laughed and became so open and friendly. He would join in my raucous chorus of "Trick or treat!" and never even falter. I never saw David so happy and so free! It was like the weight of the world had been lifted. In a way, I suppose it had been.

It amazed me, and, even as a small child, I realized that wearing a mask allowed people to see behind all the things that my brother's disabilities masked. They saw him as a real kid, something I rarely saw people consider him to be. Everyone usually saw him as everything that was wrong with him: his difficulty walking, his difficulty talking, his inability to process things quickly or use small motor control. But that night—that special, sacred night—no one saw those things. They saw the real kid since that little plastic mask he wore covered the one they always saw. And for the first time in my conscious memory, I got to lay down my boxing gloves and greet the world with open arms.

Looking back, those years went by too quickly. By the time we were too old to trick or treat, the world had changed, and I had found some friends that may have been uncertain around my brother but they loved me enough to love him, too. The moments I got a reprieve from the world were easier to find, even if they lasted only briefly. They were never the real relief those crisp Halloween nights offered, but I learned to make do. My brother's relief was harder to find and never quite as truly freeing. As years passed, he seemed to draw farther and farther into himself. Some say it was the progression of the disease. I was never quite so sure. It seemed to me that never having the chance to show the world what lay in his soul would have been enough to make any man lock his heart and mind away from the world. Or maybe that is just a reflection of my own experiences. I don't know.

No matter how old I got, or how many friends knew not to cross me when it came to my brother, I always lived on guard. You see, David was my everything. He was my child as much as he was my brother, and I would have readily laid down my life for his. I still would if he were still here. Yet, every year, those orange plastic pumpkins re-appear, and the memories flood back.

So, today I am grateful for plastic pumpkins, the symbol of my brother's only nights of freedom. Those merry adventures we took year after year, hand in hand. I will never forget them. Those crooked, black grins on those orange Halloween pumpkins will always be my reminder. And I am thankful that now my brother feels that freedom every minute of every day as he dances and sings on the streets of Heaven. What a wonderful reward for a life so long and hard! And, one day, I plan to dance those streets with him hand-in-hand as our few nights of reprieve will be swept away and replaced by an eternity of celebration.

Day 3: What are you thankful for today?

Day 4: Today I am thankful for a hand-me-down sewing machine.

Years ago, I studied to be a therapist. I worked on my master's degree while I planned my marriage and then while I was pregnant with my kids. Eventually, I did receive my Master of Arts in Professional Mental Health Counseling and even had enough hours to cover the Marriage and Family Therapy coursework as well. I never really put that degree to use on my own, but my practical hours were well-spent, studying under an amazing therapist named Paula. She had over twenty-five years of experience and taught me more in six months than I learned in four years of classes. She taught me how to put my ability to read people to good use, nailing diagnoses time and time again. She wasn't scared to tell it like it is, and she showed me that there is always more than one way to approach a problem. Most of all, she taught me that taking good care of yourself is just as important as taking care of all the things you have to do and other people expect you to do.

At the beginning of every session Paula and I shared, she asked clients what they were doing to take good care of themselves. She always encouraged the people we worked with to have a hobby. It seemed like a good idea, at least when I applied it to everyone else. I never could see how I was supposed to apply it to myself. After all, I had an eight-month-old little girl, was pregnant with my son, was working part-time with her, and was going to school for my master's degree. When would a new mom have time for a hobby? I mean, I never even slept. What was I supposed to do? I couldn't just say, "Sorry. I have to go paint for a while. I know I had less than an hour's sleep last night and have to leave for school in thirty minutes, but I have to take care of myself." It just seemed impossible.

Time went by, and the kids got older. My schedule, of course, never got any easier since no mom's schedule is ever easy, but I think I got more used to it. Unfortunately, my health took a down turn, and life got more chaotic. Although I had a little more time on my hands, I seemed to have less focus and more trouble finishing things. I also realized that there was just something else I wanted in my life. I was a good mom, at least as far as I could tell, and my life seemed to revolve around my family as many women's lives do. But I just felt like something was missing. It took me a long time to realize that what was missing was time for me. After all my excuses, I realized that Paula was right. I needed to take care of me, and that included finding something that was just for me. So, I started praying and trying out things I liked to do.

I spent time painting, but it was just not what I needed. I tried writing, but I ended up getting writer's block from my huge desire to methodically write every day. I started reading more but then had so many novels going that I felt like my brain would explode. I have never been a sports girl, so that option was a no-go on my list, not to mention that it is hard to run when you can hardly walk some days. I even tried puzzles, but the kids just *had* to help. It felt like everything I tried seemed to backfire. In the end, the answer to my prayers came in an unexpected place. A hand-me-down sewing machine.

Several months ago, I asked my mom about borrowing her sewing machine to possibly try and make a few simple things for the kids. She readily agreed. I had my own machine, but it was very, very old. My great-grandmother's to be precise. And it had broken down years before, actually while I was working with Paula. So, one day in July, while visiting my mom, I loaded up the car and brought her sewing machine home. I even brought a box of old fabric from my mother's and my aunt's collections. The sewing machine was, in fact, my aunt's. She had obtained it at a yard sale, and since she had several, she had lent the machine to my mom who had in turn lent it to me. Thus, down a winding road, the hand-me-down machine came into my possession. And what a blessing it has been.

The evening it arrived at our home, I sat down and began to fiddle and fidget with the machine. It had been years since I had a working machine, and I had a lot of re-learning to do. All the parts were supposedly the same but much, much more modern that the ancient black steel Singer I was accustomed to working. Two broken needles later, I decided I might not have been meant to sew anyway. A week passed, and I found some new needles at an affordable price and went home to make something. Several hours of pushing and prodding produced two more broken needles but little else save my dwindling sanity. But I was determined, for some reason, to figure it all out.

When my parents came over for my daughter's birthday, I conned my mother into looking at the machine. A needle later, she had it fixed, and all my insanity seemed to be worth it. That very night I sat down to work. Of course, both kids wanted to try their hand at it. Two baby doll blankets later, it was time for bed, and my dreams of crafty creativity were squashed once more. Yet something kept telling me to give it a try. The next day, I did just that.

I had seen a little girl at church wearing a dress that looked like a pillow case my grandmother had once had. I had found a reasonably-sized piece of material, and after holding it up to Diddle to see if it might fit, I decided to give it a try. I turned and twisted. I rummaged for pins and thread. I reloaded the bobbin and replaced the thread. I reset the stitch, and then I turned it back to where it was just to be safe. Thirty minutes of busy work passed, and I finally sat down to sew. I pressed the knee pedal, a totally new experience, and began to sew. Crooked more than straight, my lines of stitches paraded across the fabric. I turned the cloth and brushed back the hair from my eyes. I stitched and stitched. And, at long last, I produced a daffodil-edged pillowcase dress. A simple gold ribbon was run through the neck, and it was finished.

Diddle ran to try it on, and the sight of something I had made with my own two hands filled me with a happiness I had not known in years. No drawing or poem ever compared with the feeling of creation I felt right then. It was amazing. Absolutely amazing.

Since that fateful August day, I have made sleeping bags for baby dolls, curtains, pillow cases, and baby doll clothes. They aren't perfect by any means. They aren't even usually straight. But they are mine. Products of my own hand and my own mind, a gift I had never realized I missed but certainly realize now. I discovered that Paula was right.

Day in and day out, we go about our daily grind—working, eating, and sleeping. So many times, we push ourselves aside, saying we're too tired or too busy to do something we would like to do. It seems like the people who use those excuses are the ones who need the break most. It's when we are at the end of our ropes, when the world seems its heaviest, that each of us needs a retreat. We need something to do to make us feel special and capable and productive. We need to feel a sense of achievement, knowing that even though the list of things we must accomplish is long, we are capable of success. It doesn't have to be something huge or time-consuming. It just needs to be something we can do on our own, no strings attached to anyone or anything other than ourselves. The resulting satisfaction is worth more for our soul than we can ever imagine.

Day 4: What are you thankful for today?

Day 5: Today I am thankful for pancakes.

I can't cook. I know many women say that and are actually pretty good cooks. I, however, am not. When Mom was cooking when I was a child, I was rarely interested. I watched from time to time, but domesticity really didn't hold much charm for me. Getting assigned to do the dishes as a chore in third grade sealed the deal. Sticking my hands in that dirty water shrouded by greasy bubbles and the smell of leftover food made me queasy—green to the point that I decided I would spend my life trying to do anything other than cook. For many years, I succeeded.

When I moved out on my own, I had to fend for myself. Although I was a whiz at making a pack of instant grits and a piece of dry toast from the toaster, I had little skills in the kitchen. Sure, I could make a cake from a box or a batch of brownies with a fair amount of success. Directions usually worked okay for me in the baking field, but putting together a casserole or creating something edible from the remnants of a week's worth of meals was just way beyond my comfort zone. I lived on Lean Cuisines and boxed macaroni with the occasional can of corn snuck in. I called my Mom every time I tried to cook something more complex. By more complex I mean baking a can of biscuits or attempting to cook vermicelli. Heaven forbid I ever try to make a meat for someone. Being primarily a vegetarian, I couldn't fathom cooking meat much less figuring out how to turn it into anything other than a hockey puck. My mother remained patient with me, talking me through the steps as I cooked, sometimes spending an entire hour or more on the phone helping me make a meal.

By my mid-twenties, I decided to make an effort to learn how to cook on my own. Not only had I run out of vegetarian Lean Cuisines to try, but the three I ate were beginning to add new meaning to the word redundant. Frozen bean burritos and rice-cooked-ten-ways at the restaurant I worked at were even getting old. I began to search everywhere I could for information about how to cook. I watched the guys at my job working in the kitchen. I cornered my grandparents and wrote down their recipes on notebook paper I kept folded in a box in my kitchen. I tried to memorize temperatures and times for cooking. My mom even wrote down recipes for me and got my aunts to do the same. I was sure that I would one day be a great cook. I was amazingly deluded.

By the time my husband and I got married, I had nearly eight years of experience cooking for myself—more if you count the days and nights of fast food when I was away at college—and all of them bad. Luckily the way to his heart wasn't through his stomach, or he never would have loved me enough to marry me. I cooked here and there and made lots of frozen, ready-made meals. Once I got pregnant, however, I hated the smell of cooking food and almost gave up cooking for good. I would struggle through, gagging and sticking my head in the freezer to try and keep from getting sick. Why I thought that helped, I don't know. I do know that my cooking skills seemed to worsen rather than improve. I began to doubt that I would ever be successful at being a wife or mother. I mean, weren't moms supposed to be the best cooks on the planet?

After my first child was born, I tried to get by very similarly to the way I had before she came. Sandwiches and frozen meals with a few meals thrown in I made by following step-by-step directions seemed to be sufficient. When my son came along a year later, my doubts re-emerged. Hub was a picky eater from day one, and picky eaters and bad cooks don't mix well. He couldn't, and still can't, help it. He has a very sensitive sense of taste, and strong flavors make him physically sick. He will try things, but if the taste is too much he gets physically sick, so I had to learn to adjust my cooking even more. Unfortunately, burned food falls into the strong taste category, and meal time was a real challenge for well over a year.

This may not seem like a big crisis to many people. Friends told me to develop a routine and stick with it, cooking the things the kids would eat and I knew how to make. The problem was I still couldn't really cook even the things I knew how to cook. I burned tater tots, charbroiled chicken nuggets, blackened macaroni, and flambéed lima beans. You name it, I could ruin it. How my family ever ate a meal was beyond me. Love and hunger are still the best answers I can come up with, and a husband who knew how to cook a good bit helped. I tried new things, attempted to use my common sense to determine when things were ready, and began to experiment with the crockpot. Finally, on a Saturday evening a few years back, I decided to make a breakfast meal for dinner. It had been one of my favorite types of meals as a kid, and I had all the ingredients in my cabinet to make a good meal.

My kids saw all the boxes and bottles on the counter and took off running, screaming, "Run for cover! Hide! Hide! Mom's cooking tonight!" Yes. Most kids would say, "What's for dinner, Mom?" Mine would scream and run in the other direction. They didn't mean it to be mean. After all, if you were used to the smoke alarm going every time your mother picked up a spatula, you might develop a fear of your mother cooking, too. Still, it just seemed to reinforce my own self-doubts about cooking.

Discouraged and dejected, I began to cook. Pancake after pancake I flipped and flapped. A twelve-pancake stack looked just about right. I set the table, and we all sat down to eat. Everyone passed the plate of pancakes and took one to try. I have to say, even I was nervous. As they all began to taste, something magic happened. They smiled. Everyone seemed to like the pancakes. Even Hub! I cut into mine quickly and took a bite. Delicious! What an amazing surprise. Not burnt, not broiled, not blackened. They were actually good. The kids were grabbing for seconds before I even finished my second bite. Everyone was so busy eating they forgot to talk, a rare occasion at my little house. And when the meal was over and everyone was stuffed full, they all thanked me and told me I made the best pancakes ever. Hooray!

Don't get me wrong. I had cooked pancakes before, but never like that night. And, as a result of my little cooking success, that very evening I changed my mind about cooking. I realized I didn't have to be the best cook to feed my family. I also realized that it felt really great to finally have them want to eat my cooking. I realized that maybe part of my failure as a cook was my own self-doubt coming out as a self-fulfilling prophesy. I believed I couldn't cook, and so I couldn't. That single successful night, when my kids and my husband rushed for seconds and thirds was just enough to make me think maybe I had been wrong. And that tiny doubt about my self-doubt was enough to break the cycle of failure.

Since that night, I have burned many a meatloaf and blackened many a muffin bottom, but I have also successfully fed a family of four. My kids are growing, and my husband and I are far from starving. And, to add to it, my attitude has changed. I know I will never be a Martha Stewart or Rachel Ray, but I have come a long way from Lean Cuisines and frozen bean burritos. And now, every couple of weeks when we have a breakfast dinner, I get to hear my kids cheer for Mom's Famous Flapjacks, a sound so much more pleasant than them running and screaming in fear. And all it took was one little moment of happiness to turn around a lifetime of doubt and disinclination. Hooray for pancakes!

Day 5: What are you thankful for today?

Day 6: Today I am thankful for a DVD player.

Many years ago, when I first moved out on my own, I made the decision to not pay for cable or satellite TV. I only had a few shows I ever watched, and in my mind, paying money for something that I would mindlessly surf my way through hour after hour seemed wasteful. Besides, when my parents had finally broken down and gotten cable, the only thing I ever really enjoyed watching was old black and white movies with my dad. By the time I was on my own, I had my own VCR, and every neighborhood had a video store where I could rent a movie and keep it for a week at an affordable price. I also had plenty of my own that I watched repeatedly. *Twister* was my all-time favorite study movie. I watched it whenever I studied for a test in college. Needless to say, I knew every line and cinematography error by heart.

Time moved on, and, by the time my kids came along, I had my very own DVD player and a vast collection of movies, both new and old, to entertain myself. *Twister* stayed in my collection, renewed by the transfer to disc, and it continued to accompany my study sessions throughout grad school and even as I planned lessons when I taught school. I still couldn't see the point in buying cable. I just didn't have a TV show I couldn't live without, and I still needed the extra money. But, I was so very glad to have that DVD player. Especially when the babies came along.

When Diddle was born, I was the typical nervous mom. Every hiccup and burb was cause for alarm. To make things worse, I had made the "healthy choice" and decided to nurse, but my milk never came in. And when I say never, I mean never. I had never gone into labor nor had a contraction on my own—even 24 hours after my water had broken—so why I was surprised by this unusual turn of events I just don't know. But I was. Not even the doctors expected it. They kept telling me to keep trying. I saw a lactation specialist while we were in the hospital—time and time again. After our three days in the hospital and a trip for Diddle to the NICU later, I was using a feeding tube attached to my breast to help try and supplement Diddle's food. I was determined to breastfeed. The doctors were so supportive of this decision, I was so blinded to any idea other than I could do it that I kept trying and trying.

By the time we got home from the hospital, I was exhausted. My lack of milk left the baby constantly hungry. And fussy. And over-tired. And hungry some more. I didn't know what to do. Everyone had told me to stick it out and by the third or fourth day I would have more milk than I could imagine. That third night of Diddle's life, however, seemed like the nine millionth, and I thought I may never see the day when my child would stop crying. Every thirty minutes to an hour I had to nurse. As each hour passed, I felt more and more like I would lose my mind. Right breast and feeding tube, left breast and none. Right breast and no feeding tube, left breast and feeding tube. Over and over on eternal repeat. There was no time to sleep. My husband had to return to work the next day, and off to bed he went. I was so jealous watching him walk up that flight of stairs to darkness and quiet and more than ten minutes of uninterrupted sleep, I threw daggers at him with my eyes.

And then I was alone.

I couldn't stand the feeling of isolation that seemed to be drowning me. I walked over to the TV and turned it on. I found *Pretty Woman* and put it in the DVD player. And so it began….

It was nine o'clock at night, and my life began to take on a rhythm all its own. Well, actually not all its own. It took on the rhythm of *Pretty Woman*. "Wild One" blaring as Julia Roberts zipped up her thigh-high boots marked the first breast with feeding tube. The lobby of the hotel and Julia's run in her non-existent pantyhose marked second breast, no feeding tube. A bad shopping spree later meant burping, a clean diaper, and a new burp cloth. A dinner date, a love scene, and a polo match later, I was looking at a few minutes rest. I would be woken up about the time Julia got dressed for the opera. With any luck, I'd be back to sleep by the time she discussed Cinderella with her roommate, only to be awakened about the time Richard Gere drove in on his white limo to save the day and end the movie. From there, the cycle started all over again. And again. And again. And again.

At the time, it seemed like I was just trying to watch the entire movie. I told myself that if I just kept playing the movie over and over that I would eventually see it all the way through. It may have been true. After all, it was my determination that had me still trying to breastfeed the baby, so determination making me replay a movie dozens of times over and over seemed no less logical. I loved that sweet little bundle of baby more than anything on earth. There was absolutely nothing I wouldn't do for her, so replaying *Pretty Woman* again and again didn't seem like a crazy thing at all. At the time. By the nine o'clock in the evening on day four of Diddle's life, I had attempted to watch *Pretty Woman* twelve times. I've read that after eleven times something becomes a habit. I think in this case it was true.

Another long night passed and another long day. Twelve more attempts to watch *Pretty Woman* came and went. That poor little DVD player hummed and hummed and rattled and hummed. It worked nonstop to keep me in rhythm, and to keep that poor hungry baby somewhat fed. By halfway through that fifth night, however, I could no longer deny that I was not going to have milk to feed the baby. I broke down. I cried and wailed as much as that hungry little baby. Probably more. I felt like a huge failure. A waste of a mom. I couldn't even feed my own child. I was crushed, but I knew that I had to do what was right for my child. I woke Patrick up at three in the morning and asked him to make a bottle for the baby. He used the formula I had been using to supplement during breastfeeding and filled a bottle we had luckily gotten for when I would be at school. Four ounces of formula later, the baby stopped crying. She stopped screaming. And she went to sleep. Julia hadn't even made it to the lobby yet, and the baby was asleep! I burst out crying all over again.

As days passed, that little DVD player hummed and hummed. It kept me going and kept my rhythm steady. As the baby got more and more used to having the bottle and more and more full, I saw less and less of *Pretty Woman.* A couple weeks later, *Pretty Woman* was replaced by *Twister* as studying became a part of life again. Soon *Twister* was replaced with *Teletubbies* and glistening baby eyes that watched in awe. And then Hubby was born and *Pretty Woman* re-emerged. That little DVD player hummed and rattled round the clock for three months as that hungry baby ate every two hours. Again, I had no milk, but this time I was prepared from the start. I started him on formula in the hospital, and he drank two ounces every two hours from thirty minutes after he was born. The nurses couldn't believe it. The doctor said that since Hub was half-grown when he was born that it made complete sense. By four days old, he was drinking three to four ounces every two hours. Seeing how much Hub ate, I felt horrible for how hungry Diddle must have been with so little food in her stomach. My feelings of failure for not having milk were replaced by feelings of failure for not having realized it sooner. Luckily, she was healthy and happy once I did come to my senses.

Today, that little DVD player still rattles and hums. It has kept me company on many a late night working. It has allowed me to decide what my children see on TV, even the commercials. It has been a comforting whir on sleepless nights and entertainment on rainy days. I am thankful for all of those things. Every time I press that little stop button, however, I can't help but remember the weeks and weeks that I never had the chance to do just that. So today I am thankful for how that little DVD player helped me get through those long, new-mommy nights watching *Pretty Woman*.

"Be glad for all God is planning for you. Be patient in trouble, and prayerful always." Romans 12:12, *The Living Bible*

Day 6: What are you thankful for today?

Day 7: Today I am thankful for bench swings.

On this blustery fall day, I am thankful for a bench swing. Several years ago, my in-laws bought me a bench swing as a graduation present. It is a dark grey, metal-framed swing with a canopy over the top. The canopy can move forward or backwards to block the sun as you swing, although most days at our house in the fall it is almost vertical from the strong winds.

I've seen a lot of memories made from that swing. I watched my kids as toddlers from that swing, playing in their little plastic playhouse as they held pretend tea parties or played peek-a-boo through the windows. I watched from that swing as Hub and Diddle played in piles of leaves or rode their tricycles. One of my favorite memories, however, wasn't actually seen from the swing but rather seen on it. The adventure of Diddle and Hub's Mayflower Voyage.

It happened about a year ago, when Diddle was in kindergarten and Hub was still pretending he didn't want anything to do with school. It was a blustery fall day much like today. My husband Patrick and I had come outside with the kids after dinner for a little time outside. The kids were running and playing, and Patrick and I were talking and walking around the front yard with the dog. Diddle was complaining that they didn't have anything to play, and Hub was arguing that there was always something to do. After several minutes debate, the kids decided to play pilgrims. Patrick and I heard them and stopped by a big maple tree several yards away from them to watch and be amazed.

The kids climbed up on the swing, grabbing hold of the bars at each side and hoisting the main sail, or rather flipping the canopy to the back of the swing. Hub was at the helm, close to the front stoop. He grabbed the imaginary steering wheel and held on tight, calling to Diddle, "It's a rough trip! The waves are getting bigger!"

"Watch out, Myles Standish! We can do it! We must ride the Mayflower to the new world!" Diddle called back.

Back and forth, the bench swing Mayflower rocked along the choppy waters of the invisible Atlantic. Those two tiny pilgrims swung that ship as fast as they could on that cool autumn night. Diddle held on to her end of the boat as Hub swung on towards land. They continued to talk, sharing stories of the hardships the Pilgrims endured on the Mayflower and the sickness and suffering that continued once they found land. Those two little pretend Pilgrims swung and swung, back and forth, rocking on towards their destination. They pulled their coats in tight against the crisp autumn wind and pressed on as the maple leaves flew around them like an orange and brown rain storm. Hub held tight to his pretend steering wheel with one hand and held the swing with the other. Diddle held on tight to the rocking Mayflower. At long last, she lifted her invisible telescope to her eye.

"Land ho, Captain Standish!" Diddle cried.

"We've reached Plymouth Rock! We will go to the land and look for a place to live," Hub declared.

Precariously, they maneuvered along the length of the bench swing, walking across the still-moving Mayflower with hands held tightly to the metal seat's back. Diddle and Hub patiently awaited the end of their trip, holding on tightly as the Mayflower stopped rocking and slowed to the point that they could depart. Hub stepped down first. He reached up his hand to help his sister.

"It was such a long trip, Myles Standish! Many of us are sick, and we are all hungry. How will we find food?" Diddle asked as she stepped off the bench swing ship.

Hub looked around with his hand above his eyes, squinting as if to see some magical answer to her question.

"I see an Indian," Hub announced. "We will ask him. Let's go!"

The two weary Pilgrims left the side of the Mayflower and traveled across the wilderness of a leaf-covered driveway towards my husband and me. They stood before us, huddled together with jackets pulled tight around them. Hub pointed up to Patrick.

"Hello, big Indian man," Hub said in clipped words loudly.

"How," Patrick answered, crossing his arms across his chest and nodding.

Hub looked up at him in exasperation.

"Daddy, that is an Indian from Peter Pan. You are supposed to be an Indian from the Mayflower times. They didn't say 'how.'"

"Well, what did they say?" Patrick asked.

"They said hello, Daddy," offered Diddle.

"Okay, let's do this again," Hub said. "Hello, big Indian man!"

"Hello," Patrick answered.

Hub looked impressed. Daddy was getting with the show.

"We are Pilgrims, and we have traveled a long way. Can you help us find food?"

"What kind of food do you want? Chicken nuggets?" Patrick asked.

Exasperation returned to Hub's little face. His arms went up in the air in a dramatic gesture.

"Daddy, you are supposed to be Squanto the Indian who helps the Pilgrims plant corn. We have to catch fish and put them in holes for corn to grow," Hub explained, hoping at last that Daddy would follow the invisible script and get his lines right.

"Oh, okay. I'll get it right this time," Patrick agreed.

"Hello, big Indian. I am Myles Standish," Hub announced, changing his plan of attack.

"Hello, Myles Standish. I am Squanto. Do you want me to help you plant corn?" Patrick played along.

"Yes, thank you, Squanto," pretend-Myles said happily.

Happily the three threw out pretend fishing lines and caught pretend fish. Then they used their invisible shovels to quickly dig holes. They dropped in their fish and some corn, and covered their invisible garden with invisible dirt. Diddle quickly watered it all, and miraculously pretend corn plants sprouted, grew, and produced corn in a matter of moments. Astonished, Daddy Squanto and little Myles plucked off the invisible corn as Diddle made a massive invisible feast. We all graciously accepted our invisible plates.

"Now we have to say the blessing," Hub explained. "Pilgrims loved God like us."

We all closed our eyes and bowed our heads as Hub prayed to the Lord, thanking Him for providing us with our invisible feast. With a proud heart, I ate my invisible Pilgrim feast from my invisible plate. The sleepy little Pilgrims announced that it was time for baths and bed, and we waved them off as they departed. The two little Pilgrims headed off towards the bench swing Mayflower, happily chattering about planting corn and catching fish. They climbed aboard the Mayflower and set sail again, perhaps looking for fairer weather or a place with corn already growing. As they sailed away on that blustery autumn night on a grey bench swing, I couldn't help but feel blessed at how wonderfully amazing my life was and how amazingly grateful I was for that grey bench swing, a place I could not only watch from as my children played and grew, but a place where they could explore the world.

Day 7: What are you thankful for today?

Day 8: Today I am thankful for a yard full of dead leaves.

Every fall, the inevitable happens. The days get shorter and the cold air comes, compelling the beautiful greenery of summer to change colors and fall from the trees. As these gold, orange, red, and brown leaves litter my yard, I am not grouchy or frustrated. I don't look out at them with the dread and frustration that so many people do. Sure, I don't like the back-breaking labor of raking, but I don't dread it anymore. Quite the contrary. I actually look forward to the fallen leaves and am very thankful for them. I will readily admit, however, that this wasn't always the case.

It was in the fall of 2004 that Patrick and I moved in here, and we had a good many leaves to rake from a rather large maple planted right near our front door. It was such hard work that I left the leaves from the wild cherry tree in the backyard on the ground. Luckily, the other trees had already shed their leaves or were evergreens, or we may have lost all our grass from my lack of ambition to rake. The next couple of years were the same. I raked what I had to rake and left the rest. It was hard work, and I decided that the leaves might be better left to decompose all winter, being ecologically conscious and all. Recycling and reusing, I would call it. I don't think it helped that I was pregnant one of those first falls and had a newborn the next two in a row.

That fourth year here, things changed. Not that the leaves didn't fall. Oh, they fell, and it seemed like the most leaves I had ever seen. I always thought it took trees decades to grow huge, but our yard certainly didn't adhere to that rule. The maple was huge. The pear tree was huge. The crape myrtles were huge. The apple tree was huge. And that ginormous wild cherry? Well, it was enormously ginormous. The leaves that usually took a few months to fall seemed to fall overnight that year, and, one crisp Saturday morning in October, I opened the front door to drifts of leaves piled high along the sidewalk and a solid leaf-coating on the ground and driveway. A long sigh and a head shake later, I bundled up the babies and myself and headed out to rake the leaves.

As the mother with a one-year-old and a two-year-old at the time, the prospect of a day spent raking leaves was not high on my list of good ideas. With two children that young, a mother practically has to grow a third set of arms just to keep track of those little flying feet. I was no different. By the time I hauled the kids to the storage building and retrieved the rake, I had already spun in circles four times, made eight mad dashes for falling children, and kissed a half dozen booboos. My patience was pushing the red zone. I had no idea how I was going to even get back to the front yard. Add in the rake, and I looked like some sort of contortionist trying to swing one baby from hip to hip as I walked, trade hands for the rake, and bend backwards to hold the other baby's hand since my pace was still too fast for her little feet. Needless to say, I was exhausted before I even started raking.

When I arrived in the front yard, I deposited both babies on the sidewalk and stepped into the leafy abyss to start raking. As I raked the first few strokes, the leaves piled up over two feet tall. There were tons of them. I turned around to check on the babies who were still seated on the sidewalk examining the leaves around them. I turned back to the leaves and raked a little more. Glancing back over my shoulder, I saw that the babies were still safe and sound. I stepped out further into the orange and brown void, raking ahead of me with the children safely behind me. I glanced back at the kids, but they had disappeared. Here one second, gone the next. I swung around, and there they were, waist-high in the leaves right next to me, grinning from ear to ear.

Looking down at those little leaf-covered angels, my whole heart seemed to melt. Little Hub reached down and grabbed a handful of leaves and tossed them in the air. Diddle laughed out loud at the joke. Then they both laughed, and I laughed, too. I propped the rake against the tree and sat down with them. We picked up leaves and tossed them in the air. We threw them. We waved them. We smelled them. We felt them. But most of all, we laughed and laughed and laughed some more. Over an hour passed, but still we played. Finally, coated in leaves and dirt from head to toe, we ventured inside, leaving our golden world for the day. That magical morning those sweet babies and a yard of leaves reminded me how wonderful even the simplest things in life could be. I realized that happiness isn't something we buy or are given. True happiness is something we choose and create. The babies had known that from the start, and it was a lesson I would not soon forget.

Since that day, I have not minded raking my leaves in the fall. For the three years that followed, I raked and piled and raked and piled some more. Every pile was jumped in and destroyed within minutes. My kids rolled in them, threw them, and made forts with them. These days, they still play in the leaves. Even better, they even rake them all by themselves. They pile them high and get a running start and jump! They have leaf fights and leaf showers. They have rolling races down the leaf-covered hills and contests to see who can make the biggest leaf splash. My children may come in day after day tired and dirty and covered in leaves, but I don't mind. I shake out their clothes, comb out their hair, and move on. Watching them play in those piles of dead leaves heaped around my yard makes it all worthwhile. Each evening, leaves are scattered from our front door to our mailbox, no matter how many times they were raked that day, but I don't mind that either. I choose happiness instead.

Yes, today I am thankful for a yard full of fallen autumn leaves. Those dried, brown, crumpled leaves have a purpose these days, and my children look forward to playing in them all year long. Sometimes I think I look forward to it as much as them. Those last vestiges of fall help remind me day in and out of the sound of laughter and the smiles of my children. They remind me that each day I have a choice, and I can choose to be happy. My two tiny children turned a mountain of hard work into piles of treasure. As I look out upon how wealthy I really am, I can't help but thank the Lord for all the blessings those piles of leaves represent.

Day 8: What are you thankful for today?

Day 9: Today I am thankful for a Southern accent.

Growing up in the South, I inherited many of the peculiarities of Southern speech. The /aw/ sound that somehow finds its way into words like *dog* and *log*. The /u/ sound that the letter *e* takes on in the word *the* and the letter *a* takes on when used as a word. I spent many years working on enunciation and pronunciation in my drama and speech and debate classes. I tried to learn to control my Southern roots, continually repeating "frog-dog-log" and "the sounds like tree." It worked for quite a while. When I went away to college, I was often asked where I was from because I had gotten so good at covering up my speech quirks. As I got older, however, I began to care less and less about my Southern speech patterns, especially after I quit forensics. I came to accept my peculiarities that poked through every now and then and moved on.

By the time my children came along, I had completely forgotten about doing pronunciation exercises. I was who I was, and that was Southern. As my children began to talk, I began to think that Southern speech was actually genetic. My daughter had a drawl that outsized her father's and mine put together. My son's drawl outsized my daughter's tenfold. As preschoolers, Diddle and Hub spent a day a week with their great-grandfather. For every word their father and I pronounced without an accent, Papa Charlie pronounced five with an accent. Papa Charlie truly cultivated the children's Southernisms, unwittingly, of course. Being Southern came natural to him. It was who Papa Charlie was, and he shared it with our children fully. We didn't mind in the least, and I actually began to think that listening to those little angels' words dripping with Southern sweetness was the cutest thing on Earth. It seemed as if I could no longer deny my Southern roots if I tried.

My ultimate acceptance of my Southern roots came from my children.

It started one day last fall. It had been a long day, and the kids were sitting on the living room floor drawing. Diddle was in kindergarten and just learning to write words. Hub wasn't in school yet, and it seemed quite alright with him. He was usually quite content to scribble shapes and splotches on paper while Diddle practiced coloring inside the lines. The phone rang, and I answered. The conversation was nothing extraordinary, but the noise from the TV and the chatter of children drove me to the front porch in an effort to hear. The children were fine. Diddle was still coloring, and Hub announced proudly as I was leaving that he planned to write a letter, not an easy undertaking for a child who had only written his name up until this point. Still, I figured he was probably going to scribble the lines as he always did.

Less than a minute outside talking and peering into the living room window every few seconds to check on the kids, the front door opened. Little Hub stood there with pencil and paper in hand, looking up to me. I excused myself from the conversation and asked what he needed.

"How do you spell *uh*?" he asked.

"*Uh*?" I questioned back.

"Uh-huh. *Uh*," he answered.

"*Uh*?" I asked again, quite confused.

"Yeah, *uh*. How do you spell it?" he asked, beginning to get frustrated.

"Use it in a sentence," I said, hoping to shed some light on the situation.

"Okay," he agreed. "I want *uh* cookie."

He grinned up at me happily, proud he had figured out a sentence all on his own.

"Oh, *a*," I offered in a moment of clarity.

"No, *uh*," he retorted.

"You spell it *a*," I tried to explain.

"No. Not *a*. *Uh*," he said, completely bumfuzzled.

"Yes, I know, son. You spell *uh* by writing the letter *a*," I said.

"No, Mommy. I want to spell *uh*. Not *a*. *Uh*," he snapped.

"Hub, listen to me. You spell *uh* with the letter *a*. That's all. Just the letter *a*. We pronounce it funny here and say *uh*, but the word is really *a*."

The boy was frustrated and confused. Still, with a great bit of hesitation, he accepted my explanation and returned to his letter. I am sure it was an unusual conversation to overhear for the person I was speaking to on the phone. It was an unusual one to have, for me and the boy. And it was one that neither of us would soon forget.

Months passed, and summer came. The kids still colored and drew, and they had even begun to attempt to write more. Diddle had become determined to be very good at writing, and Hub had finally become a little envious of this ability. He had given up on actually writing letters on his own since the *uh* incident, but Diddle's new desire seemed to be rubbing off on him. They had even begun having conversations about writing and reading, a welcome event in our family. One afternoon in the car, just such a conversation began.

"*C* sure is a tricky letter," Diddle announced. "*C* says /k/ and *c* says /s/. That's tricky."

"Yeah, that's tricky," Hub agreed.

"I sure am glad I don't have a tricky letter like that in my name," said Diddle.

"You do have a tricky letter in your name," Hub responded.

"No, I don't."

"Yes, you do."

"No. I don't."

"Yes. You do."

"Fine. What letter?" Diddle asked, finally giving in.

"The letter *a*," Hub answered matter-of-factly.

"Huh?" Diddle and I both asked together.

"Yeah. The letter *a* is the trickiest letter of all," Hub began. "*A* says /ā/ and *a* says /ă/, but around here *a* also says /uh/."

I nearly choked trying not to laugh. Diddle sat there looking puzzled, and Hub seemed a bit indignant that we both did not seem to readily accept his profound explanation. So I nodded as I managed to choke out that he was correct.

To this day, I can't help but smile when I listen to my children talk. I even love to hear my own Southern accent come out. I especially love listening to all the *uhs* that find their way into our daily life. These days I am thankful for those little quirks instead of conscientious about them. After all, without them I wouldn't have gotten to experience such a wonderful story. And that in itself is something to be thankful for in my book.

Day 9: What are you thankful for today?

Day 10: Today I am thankful for ladybugs.

Many, many moons ago, a local university had a project involving ladybugs. When the project was over, they let the thousands upon thousands of ladybugs free. After all, ladybugs are essentially harmless for all means and purposes. They aren't poisonous or venomous. They don't bite or sting. And they don't really harm the environment. The only bad thing about ladybugs is that they make more ladybugs and more… and more… and more…. Every year the population of those little red and black flying ladies grows and grows. And every year, more and more come to visit us.

Eight years ago when I moved to this little town, I had no idea about the ladybugs. I had seen them in passing as I grew up, and I had made my wishes on them as I sang their little tune.

Ladybug, ladybug,
Fly away home.
Your house is on fire
And your children are gone.

That first fall, I sang that song many times. As the weather got colder, however, I seemed to be singing it more and more. Every evening after work, I would come in to find several ladybugs had made their way inside. I would round them up, open the door, and, with a little blow, send them flying off into the evening air. A week passed by, then two. By the end of October, I was rounding up dozens a day. By the end of November, I had almost given up, especially upstairs. In the corners of the ceiling, there would be huddling masses of ladybugs, ten to twelve deep. Patrick explained to me about how the ladybugs came to be so prolific in this area and how his family had fought them for years, but I still was at a loss as to what to do.

Night after night, I would lie in bed and a few stray ladybugs would scuttle across the ceiling, me lying there wondering if they were going to fall in my mouth while I slept. There were just too many to round them all up every day. My mother-in-law suggested vacuuming them up. I had a hard time with that idea. After all, they weren't hurting anything, and I felt sorry for them. Maybe it was the song running through my head, making me feel like their houses were on fire and their children were gone. Maybe it was just my love of animals and my desire to save them, even though I didn't even know what they ate. It was depressing. By Christmas, I gave up, and I vacuumed up the few remaining bugs before starvation and dehydration turned them into orange polka-dotted corpses lining the crevices where the carpet met the wall.

The next fall brought the lady bugs back in droves. I started autumn freeing a dozen or more a day, chanting my little song.

Ladybug, ladybug,
Fly away home.
Your house is on fire
And your children are gone.

By December, I had resigned to the vacuum. Hundreds upon hundreds flooded the house, and the corners of the ceilings in all rooms were mounded day in and day out. It didn't seem to matter how many I let go, they all seemed to come back. It didn't seem to matter how many I vacuumed, there were always hundreds more to take their place. It seemed like an act performed in futility. Those little black spotted bugs were determined to invade my home, and I was growing weary trying to free them.

Years have passed, and the ladybugs have just kept coming. Their population has just kept growing. The more I set free, the more invade. By the end of last fall, I had given up on the idea of freeing them. It seemed as if the vacuum cleaner was meant to be their fate. As this fall began, I was so disappointed to see that their numbers had yet again increased. I was fed up, at my wit's end, and had been pushed to my very edge. The past few months have been a continual battle, me freeing and them invading. I finally reached my breaking point. *Why do these bugs keep invading my home? What is it about this place that they can't seem to leave? Go home, ladybugs! Seriously! Go home!*

Today it hit me. They couldn't. Not because of the rhyme I have chanted time and time again over the last eight years that claimed their homes were burned but because they had no home. The swarms of thousands of ladybugs clinging to my roof and exterior walls want to be here because they have no home of their own. They want to be inside my home where there is warmth and safety. Where there is a dry place to lay your head and a quiet place to rest. They want to be inside my home because they want and need a home.

I never realized how lucky I am to have a home. I've said I was grateful time and time again. I've prayed to keep our home or in thanks for our home, but I never really understood how truly fortunate I am. My home doesn't move; it stays right here. I am not forced to travel miles upon miles to find a safe place to stay. My home is warm and dry. I don't have to scrounge for sticks, brush, and broken limbs to make a fire, and I don't have to worry about being soaking wet if it rains. My home is safe. I can come inside and lock the doors and live with relative peace of mind that I will wake up tomorrow without being harmed through the night. My home is welcoming and loving. We smile and laugh and love here. It isn't the biggest home, but is by far not the smallest. It's old and little, and there are many things that need to be done. But it is a home, and it is mine. Those little ladybugs want to be here because they, too, want a home. How lucky am I that they want to share mine?

Day 10: What are you thankful for today?

Day 11: Today I am thankful for miracles.

Today I am thankful for miracles, and, yes, they do happen in everyday life. I know it may not seem like it, but miracles happen all the time. Sometimes they are little things like the sun coming out on a rainy day when you had big plans outside. Sometimes they are bigger. The miracles I am thankful for today are the bigger kind.

Nineteen years ago, on the eleventh of November, it was a regular Friday night. I had been at school all day and gone in to work at four o'clock. I was scheduled to be early-out on hostess, a little favor on the busiest night of the week in any restaurant. Saturday morning I was scheduled to host in my home store, a three-hour drive away. It seemed crazy to commute every weekend from college to work in my hometown, but it was much more profitable than working at the restaurant I worked at all week while in school. I even had plans that night, a movie and popcorn with a friend from the university. I couldn't wait to leave work.

When the first staff cuts were made that night, it was after eleven. It had been a wild, jam-packed night, and I was beyond ready to leave. I had been in class all day before I came in, and I had an early morning ahead of me. I went to ask the manager to walk me out to my car, but he was wrapped up in conversation with some regulars at the bar. He told me to wait. I waited about ten minutes and got frustrated. I told him I was leaving, but I don't know that he even heard me. My car was parked on the side of the building, not the back, and it was under a streetlight, so I wasn't too worried about the twenty-yard walk from the front lobby.

I took off out the side entrance and headed towards my car. It was getting really cold, and my blue short-sleeved shirt was not really working to keep me warm. I wrapped my arms around my chest and quickened my pace. I had my gotten my keys out while I waited inside, and I played with the quarter-size tire-shaped base that the key ring actually popped on and off. Cars whizzed by on the busy boulevard, and their quiet roar seemed to be muffled by the freezing wind blowing through the giant trees that surrounded the side and back parking lots. About half-way across the parking lot, I noticed a man in a hoodie, smoking at the back of the building.

"Hey," the man said, looking up at me from under his hoodie.

I half-waved and answered, "Hey."

I veered off to the left, headed for my car. Behind me, muffled steps became pounding thunder claps. Before I could turn, the pounding steps were upon me and an arm wrapped around my neck. I tried to look around, but the arm around my neck forced my head upwards. I could see the crowbar as it crashed into my forehead.

The next thing I remember was coming to, lying on the cold cement with my head placed behind my front tire. The man in the hoodie was beside me trying to force a key into the car door. All I could think was that I needed to get out from under the car. I knew if he succeeded in opening the door I would be dead. I had been ten feet from the car when I blacked out, and I had no doubt in my mind that my head hadn't been placed behind that tire on accident. Slowly, centimeter by centimeter, I tried to slide out from under the car. I didn't want him to see me, and I tried not to move any body part more than a breath's height so as to not draw attention. I made it about four inches before he turned to see if I had come to. I closed my eyes and held my breath, terrified. It was too late though. He had seen I was conscious.

"Which key is it?" he demanded, waving my dorm key at me.

"I don't know," I answered in complete honesty.

"Tell me what key it is!" he hissed at me.

"I don't know," I repeated.

He threw the key on the ground, and I noticed that my key ring had fallen apart. Keys were scattered on the ground, glinting in the streetlight. He grabbed my purse and opened it. He rummaged through it, digging for my wallet. He pulled out my ATM card. He began demanding my pin number.

"I don't remember it," I said.

"You're lying! What is it?" he demanded.

"I don't know. I don't have any money."

"Give me the pin number!" he demanded, rifling through my wallet.

He pulled out the twenty dollar bill I had folded in my change purse and jammed it in his pocket.

"You're taking me to the bank. Get up!" he ordered.

I slid my head the rest of the way out from under the car, and he grabbed me before I could stand and run. He wrapped his arm around my neck.

"You're taking me to the bank. Come on! Which key is it?"

"I don't know. I don't know the number. My bank has cameras. I don't know the number. I have no money."

The stream of sentences ran from my mouth. Anything I could say to deter him, to throw him off, to hold out until I could come to my senses. It didn't work. I was so panicked I just kept repeating the same jumbled mess over and over.

"Shut up, you lying white b——!" he hissed as he hit me with the crowbar again.

It didn't last as long that time. I came to as he was pulling me to my feet, his arm wrapped tight around my neck again. As he pulled me towards the wooded ravine that bordered the side parking lot, a car came by. I tried to yell for help, but the car kept going. The yellow streetlight was blinding bright against the pitch black of the woods ahead.

"People will see you. People will know. They'll look for me," I said, trying to reason with him.

He beat my head into a tree. I fell to the dirt. I had enough sense to know that death lay ahead, and I began to plead to God. *I can do it, Lord. I can do it. Just let me live. I can do it. I can bear whatever you give me. Just please, God, let me live. I'm only nineteen, God. I have so much life to live. I can bear it, Lord. Just please let me live.*

I continued trying to reason with my attacker. He continued to beat me and curse me. He rammed my head into roots and rocks, over and over again. As I slid and slipped down the black wooded slope, he threw me into trees and bashed me with the crowbar. In a bruised and battered heap, I landed at the base of the ravine. He hit me once more as he ripped off my pants. My words would no longer come, no voice left to make the sounds. Only tears, silent as the grave.

Please, God, please. I can do it. I can bear it. Just let me live. I'm only nineteen. Just let me live. I can carry this. I can. I don't want to die. I'm only nineteen.

The angry man cursed me as he raped me, his hand tight around my throat. He squeezed and squeezed until the breath was gone. I looked down at my body, still pleading with God to let me live. Moments passed, looking down at the gruesome scene. The angry man stood and grabbed my pants, leaving me lying there half-naked on the dank, dead leaves. With a rush, the world came back. I lay there terrified, as I listened to the man climb the ravine. In the distance I saw his flashlight scanning the area at the top of the ravine. I waited for what felt like hours but was really only minutes, and I started to creep across the damp, cold ground. I clawed and grabbed, pulling myself up the slippery slope, trying to be as quiet as a mouse. I peered out of the thick trees, praying he was gone. I saw no one. My pants lay a few feet away in a wrong-side out pile. I crawled out into the light and grabbed my pants. I pulled them on in seconds and took off to the restaurant and safety.

I made a deal with God that night. If he performed a miracle, I would bear the weight of that night forever. It was a deal I have never regretted. God gave me life, and I gave Him my word that I would bear the weight of that horrible night. Two years later, I developed an early form of cervical cancer. It was luckily found early on, but for years I battled with it. Procedure after procedure, paired with the scar tissue from the assault, virtually destroyed my chances at having children. At the age of twenty-two, the doctors told me my chances of having children were 99.9% in favor of me not being able to have them. I had had my cervix removed in the fight against the cancer, and the doctors told me that even if the baby found a place that wasn't scar tissue to adhere that I would never be able to carry the baby past a month or so. I had never realized I wanted children until the doctors said I could never have any. My heart was broken, but I kept my faith. I was still alive, despite all the things that had happened to try and end me.

At twenty-five, I was again battling the cancerous cells. The doctors informed me that I would probably need a hysterectomy within the year. They offered me the chance to try and have a baby then or never. A procedure had been developed that might allow the doctors to place supports in my uterus to help me carry a baby, although they warned me it had only a small chance of success. I also ran the risk of the cancer spreading and possibly growing faster if I tried for a baby. Being single at the time, I decided to fight the cancer. Even if I had been brave enough to try, I did not know if I could handle losing a baby I had selfishly tried to bring into the world by miscarriage. I resigned myself to childlessness. Procedure after procedure, I beat back the cancerous cells, and I even kept my uterus.

At the age of thirty I was married. For eight years, I had been told I would never have children. For eight years, I had believed it. My family believed it. My friends believed it. We had all heard it so many times that we had no reason to think otherwise. It was not a subject any of us talked about anymore because it just didn't seem worth talking about. In my mind, I reasoned that God have given me life, and that was why I couldn't give life myself. It wasn't like I thought God was keeping score. More like I felt like it was fair. The damage from that night was why I couldn't have kids. To me, it seemed like it was just part of my deal. I had agreed to bear it, and so I did.

But something happened. On the eleventh anniversary of my assault, on the eleventh day of the eleventh month, I became pregnant with my first child, Diddle. When I went to the doctor two weeks later, everyone was floored. They all had thought it was impossible, too. I was warned not to get too excited until I made it through the first trimester. I reluctantly agreed. I was scared out of my mind. For eight years, I had believed I would never have children. For eight years, I had accepted that not having children was just part of my deal with God. I was wrong.

I went on to have a very healthy pregnancy. Then four months after I had Diddle, I was pregnant with Hubby. My body held on to those babies tighter than anyone had ever thought possible. But it was. The doctors teased me that I had gone from sterile to being a Fertile Myrtle. I was quite happy with that diagnosis.

Looking back I realize that on the day I dreaded most each year, I was given not only my own life but the life of my child, as well. I realize that God doesn't necessarily make deals the way people do. For him, a miracle is just that—a miracle. He gave me my life when I was attacked not because I bargained with him but because he loved me and it wasn't my time to go. My bargain only benefited me. I was the one who was able to handle what had happened because I had told God and myself I could and would. Diddle was God's gift to me, and she helped me to finally fully understand that God also doesn't have to take things away from us as payment for good deeds he has done in our lives. God doesn't keep score. He's not sitting up there with a big scoreboard tallying points against us. He loves us, and some things are meant to be while others aren't. If I had never had children, it wouldn't have been because I made a bargain with God to spare my life or because I did something wrong and was being punished. A miracle is a miracle, and I had to be faced with one on two separate occasions with an insanely unusual anniversary to finally see that. A miracle is a gift, no strings attached, and I have been more than blessed by the two that I am thankful for today.

"What I want from you is your true thanks; I want your promises fulfilled. *I want you to trust me in your times of trouble, so I can rescue you and you can give me glory.*" Psalm 50:14, *The Living Bible*

Day 11: What are you thankful for today?

Day 12: Today I am thankful for time.

As Americans, we place a great deal of importance in the concept of time. We schedule our lives with it. We save it and squander it. We argue about it and try to find it. We hold onto it with all our might. Yet, somehow, it always eludes us. Time keeps moving on, and we move along with it, kicking and screaming or willingly, whatever the case may be. I choose to merely try and keep up. Some days that is harder than others, but each day is precious and worth the effort.

It's hard for me to believe I'm as old as I am. It seems like yesterday I was in elementary school, riding my bike and playing with dolls. I always heard adults talk about how time flies, but I never really understood what they meant. I knew time went quickly when you were having fun, but it still didn't seem to fly, by any means. As a child, time felt like an eternally ticking clock. Each minute seemed exaggerated, a giant booming tick on the hands of time. Days and weeks crawled by, seeming as if they would never pass. Holidays would never come, and waiting for Santa felt like it took eons. Middle school was an eternal torment, time dragging me backwards it moved so slowly. Even in high school, time moved slowly, and the future seemed so far away. During high school, I felt as if my life had hit a grand plateau. Life was looming ahead, a giant mountain full of adventure. Childhood was in the valley below, in the past, but still close enough for me to hold onto. Somehow, I never realized that time was passing right before my eyes.

Sometimes it feels as if I went from high school to being thirty and married with a child on the way. It feels as if my life actually started when the kids came, and life until that point was merely guiding me to them. Time seems to move differently since my children arrived. My aunt once told me that once you have children, each day is an eternity but each week is only a minute. She couldn't have been more correct. When my children were babies, I would feel as if I had been going nonstop for twenty years by the time I had dinner made. Managing to eat and go to the bathroom was a successful day. The days when I fit in a shower were like gold medal days, far too precious to earn only a blue ribbon. Yet, somehow, each week seemed to blow past me as if I were standing still. Months would flash by in a blink, and Diddle was a year old before I turned around. Once Hub came, all hope at keeping track was futile.

These days I can finally understand what all the grown-ups of my youth meant about time flying. To this day, I don't really know where the last six years went. I say that honestly, even though I know I must have lived it to be standing here today. It seems as if it all runs together into one eternal day. Baby days run into toddler days, and I'm not quite sure if Hub didn't come out talking and walking. It's such a blur of laughter and tears that it's hard to comprehend that each day passed separately, all on its own. Even harder to see is the future, a place that looms just out of sight beyond today. No matter how hard I try, all my tomorrows keep turning into yesterdays. I'm afraid this vicious cycle will continue until I run out of both.

It sometimes feels like most of my adult life outside of my kids is nothing but work. From overtime to unpaid time, work consumes so much of my life. The days of working nine-to-five seem like a time-faded dream, especially now that my husband's work hours change from day to day. I know that my own time often gets consumed by little jobs throughout the day that seem to fill up every nook and cranny with work. I am either working on something or preparing to work on something, and what little time I have seems to disappear before my eyes. Sometimes I have the feeling that I may look back and think that all work and no play made for a wasted life. I know in my heart that I don't want that to happen, so I have made the decision to make myself take time off at least one day a week to spend with my husband and kids. Time is fleeting, and I plan to spend the rest of my life being thankful for it rather than trying to beat it or being beaten by it.

Looking back over the time I've spent here on Earth, there have been so many important days. Birthdays, weddings, first steps, first teeth. But in the end, all the days make up one big event consisting of all of our counted minutes and hours. That event is life. Life is the sum of all our minutes, each breath measured and accounted for from birth until death. Time is our way as humans to try and keep track of life. Yet, no matter how much we schedule it, life just keeps on happening. It is our job to never take it for granted. Time keeps moving, and it is up to us to jump aboard, hold on, and do our best to enjoy the ride.

Day 12: What are you thankful for today?

Day 13: Today I am thankful for blankets.

When my little household woke up this morning, our outside thermometer read ten degrees. There is little wonder that, with such frigid temperatures, I was more than thankful for my warm bed and thick blankets this morning. Walking across the kitchen tile felt like dancing on ice cubes, and even the air inside the house had a chill. I would definitely have preferred to stay in bed buried under a pile of fluffy blankets. In fact, I would still much rather be buried under a pile of fluffy blankets. Then again, I can't think of many people who wouldn't.

Blankets have to be one of the best creations ever made. Blankets come in all shapes and sizes. Soft, little frilly ones wrap up baby girls, and blue, puppy-dog-printed ones swaddle baby boys. Fluffy pastels turn into baseballs and Barbies, leading the way to plaids and polka dots. Over time, our blankets change as we do, although some of us hang on to a few special ones along the way. In fact, one of my very favorite blankets is almost as old as me. Well, at least as old as I like to think I am.

Some thirty years ago I received a very special blanket, a quilt my grandmother made. Nanny had always been artsy. She loved crafts and ceramics. I think I spent half my childhood watching her paint wooden shapes, creating people and scenes. Nanny could take a piece of shaped wood and make the most adorable country grandmas and grandpas. I watched her and my mother paint ceramic people, and my grandmother could paint a smile so real that it looked like you could see the gleam in those little figures' eyes. I always thought that painting must be the easiest thing on the Earth because the way she did it seemed so effortless. I took up my crayons and markers and drew, believing I could one day do just what she did.

By the end of third grade, I had become fascinated by fashion. By fourth grade, I had become addicted. My art dreams had found a path of their own, and I began to see myself as an up and coming Liz Claiborne. Even more, I knew my path was to design fancy ball gowns. Of course, I think that may have had a little something to do with so many of my friends being as fascinated by fashion as I was. When we got together, there was no ball gown too amazing or stiletto too high for us to imagine. We were going to set the fashion world ablaze with our revived devotion to the hoop skirt, sweetheart fitted-top, and wide-brimmed hat. I think I must have been responsible for the destruction of a small forest by the amount of paper I used designing my gowns. When combined with my friends, we may have single-handedly been responsible for the devastation of the rain forests.

My devotion to fashion was well-known in my family. My notebooks had scribbles and scrabbles penciled everywhere. I walked around constantly with a pencil in my hand, and all it took was a pack of markers and a single-subject notebook to keep me entertained for hours. I bled dry pack after pack. Nanny saw my interest in art as something to nurture, and I know I would have given up on it many times had she not put a pencil in my hand and shoved paper in front of me. In fact, she took my love of drawing women's fashions to the next level. She made me a quilt.

The quilt was something I could never have dreamed. Nanny had taken my aunts' and my old dresses and cut them up into magnificent hoop skirts and hats. Then she had created row after row of them. She stitched them by hand onto a cream background and enclosed each lady in a pink, square border. Brown, black, and gold stitched hair hung out from beneath wide-brimmed bonnets. Twenty-four Southern Belles stood elegantly with tiny black slippers poking out beneath their ball gowns. Bell sleeves hung gracefully above hands outstretched as if waiting to accept an offer to dance. It was the most amazing thing I had ever seen, and it was even more amazing because it had been made especially for me. I loved that quilt!

Many years have passed since my Nanny made that blanket for me. It has hung in quilt shows and on walls, and it has adorned my beds for many years. Now it adorns my daughter's bed. My grandmother passed on a year and a half ago, but every time I look at that quilt it feels like she is right here with me. This blanket was a labor of love, and I am sure it took more of her spare time than I will ever know. It has stood the test of time, and its warmth is unparalleled in my book. On a day as cold as today, I am thankful for its warmth and comfort. You see, I wasn't the only one who would have rather stayed in bed today. A certain little girl I know would have much rather stayed buried underneath that blanket, too. I never imagined thirty years ago that such a thing was even possible. So, yes, today I am thankful for blankets.

Day 13: What are you thankful for today?

Day 14: Today I am thankful for books.

As a writer and an editor, I think it goes without saying that I would be thankful for books. But my appreciation for books goes beyond work or making money. In fact, you could say I love everything about books. I love the feel of the paper in my hand, the weight of the words on my palm. I love the smell of the pages: some crisp and woody, some warm and musty. I love the strength of them, the resiliency the words have to stand against time and change. And I love the comfort of them. I can return to them time and again, each time feeling something familiar but always something new as well. I especially love how they can take you just about anywhere you want to go.

Reading, for me, has been a lifelong passion. From the time I read my first book, I could never get enough of them. Sometimes I read them openly, passing the time and enjoying a little relaxation. Sometimes I read them privately, a secret escape from the weight of the world. My perfect day off would be lying in bed under a pile of blankets reading a book. That, to me, sounds heavenly. Even with an insane schedule, I can't imagine not being in the process of reading a book. There are times nowadays when it takes me a month or more to read one, but I still do it. I just can't resist. Books call to me, and I have to answer.

Beyond my love of books, I am thankful for the knowledge they have provided me. I am what some people call "book smart." If I was interested in something, I looked it up in a book. Computers weren't the thing while I was growing up, and I have never been able to break the habit of searching out a book to answer my questions. I remember trips to the library, armed with a backpack and a library card, in search of one book after another. That fantastic smell as I slid open drawer after drawer of the card catalog. The silky feel of those paper cards as my fingers sped through to the right place. Learning was a full sensory experience, and it helped make everything I learned from books all the more tangible and meaningful.

Over the years, the things I have discovered in books have accumulated. From the social construction of reality to String Theory in quantum physics, books have been my doorway to knowledge. I have a plethora of knowledge filed away in my brain, file cabinet after dusty file cabinet filled with interesting tidbits from books. Yet, I don't think I could ever consider any of that information useless. Somehow, I always seem to find a use for it, if nothing other than saying I know it. My great-aunt used to tell me that knowledge is the gift we give ourselves. Well, I have given myself more presents than I deserve.

Books are such a wonderful blessing. How amazing is it that we can read about the lives of people that lived thousands of years ago? How awesome is it that we can pick up a book and feel the feelings explorers felt as they discovered new lands? We get to travel to space, to exotic destinations, and to other galaxies while sitting at home in our pajamas. We get to fight wars without ever seeing a battlefield. We get to dance with a prince or serenade a princess. We get to climb the highest mountains and dive to the deepest depths. We get to live any life we choose. All it takes is a book.

I once read that if a person reads on hour a day, every day for a year, on a specific subject, then that person will become an expert on the subject. That's right. 365 days of reading, and you can become an expert in any field of study you choose. I have decided that my next challenge will be doing just that. I also extend that challenge to you. Isn't there a subject out there that you just can't do without? Pet care? Criminal law? The Bible? Take an hour a day and read, and next year at this time you will have accumulated enough knowledge to be an expert in that field. What will your subject be?

Day 14: What are you thankful for today?

Day 15: Today I am thankful for dogs.

Over the years, I have had several dogs, some longer than others. My dog growing up was a sweetie, a little white and grey furball named Missey. She was loyal and loving, like a Benji movie come to life. We got her from a friend of mine, and it was probably the best decision in a pet I could have ever made. She taught me how to love someone with my whole heart, a lesson I am daily grateful for having learned. She also taught me the meaning of faithfulness. Day after day, she waited for me to come home from school or work or dates. She would lie on our driveway and just wait. When I would finally show up, she would dance and jump like I was the most awesome person she had ever met.

Several years after Missey came to live with us, she disappeared. I put up signs all over the neighborhood and was worried sick. Each day, as I waited for her, I would go sit on the driveway where she always sat waiting on me. The hole in my heart was so big. I couldn't bear to imagine that what I was feeling was what she might have felt each time I went away. It was awful.

After Missey had been gone for a week, we pieced together that someone had shot her and taken her body to a landfill miles away. I was totally crushed. I lost all hope, and I decided I would never have another dog. I went out to sit on the driveway one last time, crying my heart out. As I was getting up to go inside, I noticed something coming down the street. It was her! I ran up the street and scooped her up in my arms. She was filthy and stunk, and her whole backside was covered in blood and grime. She had indeed been shot. Her entire hind quarters were littered with buckshot, but even through that she had found her way home. Her love and her loyalty was beyond anything I could have imagined. Missey lived to be around 16 years old, and she set a hard precedent for any dog to follow.

When I was 24, another dog found her way into my life. That dog was Annabel Lee. Annabel Lee was a German Shepherd and pit-bull mix, but you would never have known about the pit-bull if it weren't for her rather square lower jaw and massive squared chest. She was probably the smartest dog I have ever known. I was living in Rome, Georgia at the time, and she showed up on my doorstep one night—a scrawny, scabby runt. I fed her some bread and gave her some water and away she went. She appeared the next morning as I was leaving for work, and I swore I would keep her if she was there when I got home. When I came home, she was nowhere to be found. I was beyond disappointed. Missey had been unable to move with me. She was blind by this time and knew every inch of my parents' house by heart, and I couldn't have stood taking her away from her home. Besides, while I was away at college she had become my dad's best friend and my mom's constant shadow, and I couldn't bear to take that away from any of them. So, without the constant love of a dog, I was a little lonely. I didn't have to wait too long.

About eight o'clock that evening, I heard what sounded like scratching at the front door. I opened it up, and in walked Annabel. She sat down in the middle of the room like she owned it. My heart was gone. I took her to the vet, and they told me she was probably about two but that she was so malnourished that they couldn't tell for sure. She had mange, but it was treatable. She had also been beaten pretty badly with a crowbar, a tortuous instrument that had taken huge gouges out of her body. By our two month follow-up, Annabel weighed over ninety pounds and was mange-free, and it had become beyond obvious that she was definitely not an adult dog. She was a giant puppy. The rest, as they say, is history.

Annabel and I were like two halves of a whole. I treated her like a person, and, as much as she could, she became one. She watched TV and had an unreal fear of Arnold Schwarzenegger as Mr. Freeze in Batman. She would hide her head under her paws whenever he came on, but then watch the rest of the movie just fine. She figured out how to open the refrigerator and cabinets. She helped herself to a turkey leg one Easter and orchestrated "The Great Muffin Heist" with her friend Samson.

Annabel Lee was also adept at knocking things off the counter to eat. One night she ate an entire bag of Dum Dums. She carefully unwrapped each one, ate the candy, and then laid the stick on the paper. I'm sure she didn't want to get in trouble for making a mess, not that nearly two hundred sucker sticks and wrappers wasn't a mess. She just didn't want the sticks to get stuck in the carpet.

Another night she ate an entire bag of Hershey's kisses. The next morning my roommate stayed with her while I went to work because I was scared since dogs shouldn't eat chocolate. It didn't hurt Annabel. That crazy dog just ran in circles for an hour nonstop. She also ate most of a fifty pound bag of cat food, numerous pillows, lamp cords, at least two dozen VCR tapes, two shelves full of books (ironically she stopped at *War and Peace*, leaving me to believe it was more than she could chew), several cabinets, a wall, carpet, a pair of boots, and more Nylabones than I could count. Yes, Annabel would, and could, eat anything.

Annabel was a wonderful dog. I have more stories about her than I could ever record. Of course, after sixteen years together, it's not a surprise. I loved her very much. Watching her wither away at the hands of cancer and old age was heart-wrenching, but I would never trade our time together for anything. She stood guard over me for many years, and she ended her life standing guard over my family. It's funny, but she gave me the strength to accomplish so much just by being herself. Her devotion was proven time and again. Although I only knew her to make a move towards a human on a handful of occasions, each time was in defense of me. I trusted her with my life, and she with me. I know very few humans I could say that about. She was truly my best friend.

These days our home is guarded by Koko, a little Basset Hound/ Cocker Spaniel mix. He is a redhead like me, with freckles like me. He had been in the shelter for three months before we took him home. He is crazy and fun and the kids adore him. He is a precious dog, and we are so lucky to have him. He reminds me of how much Missey and Annabel loved me when he barks at me every time one of the kids cries. It's like he thinks I'm not moving fast enough to help them, and I like that. It lets me know he loves them. Even more, I know they love him. Growing up knowing that kind of love made such a difference in my life. I am thankful that my kids will have that same opportunity.

Day 15: What are you thankful for today?

Day 16: Today I am thankful for index cards.

When I was in school, index cards meant one of two things—a research paper or reviewing for a test. I can't begin to explain how many hours I spent writing information on index cards. It was a helpful practice, separating information into bite-size chunks. Somewhere in high school I picked up the practice from an English teacher, and it followed me through my master's degree. I would number the authors on my bibliography and put the number on each card. Then I would write a single quotation or piece of information on each card. That way I could move and re-arrange the cards in any way I needed when I was preparing to write a paper and still easily know from where the information came. It was a sure-fire way to avoid plagiarism, and probably the only effective organizational tool I ever used over and over without being told. As far as reviewing for a test, one of my best friends always made index card flashcards for every test, drilling and drilling those little flashcards until all the information stuck in her brain. I usually got the privilege of being the one to ask her the questions on the index cards, and, although it ultimately helped me study, I still dreaded them. Either way, they were helpful when it came to school.

These days index cards have a more diverse role to play in my home. They are still used for school—my children's, not mine. But they have also taken on new roles. My husband is an extremely good writer and one of the most avid readers I have ever known. I mean, this is a guy who reads Chaucer for fun. Not many people can say that. He also has a true love of Russian literature. Having gotten to know him while going to school in Russia, that kind of fits, though. One of his favorite authors is Nabokov. While reading a biography on Nabokov, Patrick discovered that Nabokov often wrote his novels out on index cards and then sorted them into the immense volumes he wrote. Finding it to be an intriguing idea, Patrick set out to do the same. When something hits him, he can be found scribing his thoughts on index cards. Needless to say, we have many piles in many locations, all of which I find incalculably fascinating and immeasurably charming. Those little piles remind me of how intelligent my husband is and add to the list of adorable eccentricities that I love about him.

Index cards are also a favorite of my children. Index cards are small and hand-sized for young children. They are also firmer then notebook paper and seem to hold up better when the kids press down too hard or erase too fervently. Index cards are also a readily available source of paper since, as I mentioned, my husband has tons of them lying around. Each day, my kids seem to find new uses for these little pieces of paper. Index cards become invitations to tea parties and notes to superheroes in thanks for keeping our planet safe. They become books of scribbled lines and signs that get taped to the wall indicating such things as parents aren't allowed in Kidtown or which direction Peter Pan should look to find his shadow. Index cards become tickets to plays the kids put on, concerts they perform, or this week's Big Game that will be held in the backyard. They become notes to Tiffany the tooth fairy asking her to please leave Hub something special, too, when Diddle loses a tooth. Index cards even become price tags and play money when it's time to play store. My kids have so many uses for them that I don't think I could even name them all, but one thing is for sure, index cards are used daily in this house.

While my husband started the plenitude of index cards in our home, I have no problem supporting this unusual habit. After all, he passed it on to our children, and it seems to have stuck. While I thought my days of flipping through index cards was finally over, it seems as if I were certainly wrong. Not that I mind. In fact, I truly enjoy it. I suppose the difference is that flipping through the hundreds of index cards my children use is so much more pleasant than index cards used to be. Those little pieces of paper now make me smile, knowing that my children are creative and intelligent, two traits for which I am beyond thankful.

Day 16: What are you thankful for today?

Day 17: Today I am thankful for tape.

Some children love bikes, and some love dolls. Some collect stickers, while others can't get enough of trains. All children seem to have something they love the best. For my son, his greatest love is tape. He uses it constantly, and not a day passes when he doesn't find a need for it. To Hub, tape is one of the greatest inventions ever made, ranking right up there with popsicles and brownies.

I can't say exactly when or how his fascination with tape began, but I can say that it has existed for the larger part of his life. Given, he is only six years old, but that just makes it seem like an even bigger percentage of time. However it may have begun, it is a love affair I am sure is far from over.

Living in the reduce-reuse-recycle era, Hub has always been conscientious about the environment. He has made it his lifelong mission to find new uses for old things. His number one ally in this mission—Tape. At age three, Hub began taping paper, straws, and used popsicle sticks together to make homemade kites and toys. By the time he was four, Hub was taping art work and other things he was proud of on the walls. On his fifth birthday, Hub got an action figure in the molded plastic, paper-backed package that so many of them come in. He refused to let us throw it away. With the help of his buddy Tape, he made it into a boat for the bathtub.

Other re-use creations by Hub include towers, toy carriers, paper flowers with drinking-straw stems, and every spy gadget you can imagine. He's even used tape to put his toys "in carbonite" like Han Solo in *Star Wars*. In reality, they were broken toys that Tape and Hub worked together to find a new use for instead of having them go to the landfill. There seems to be nothing (inedible) that Tape can't help Hub recycle.

Hub also uses tape to display things. He hangs up artwork and school work. He tapes notes to our family on the wall. He tapes cards to the wall.

He writes notes about the book he is reading and tapes them up. He creates tournaments, contests, and other sporting events for his sister and him and tapes announcements about them on the walls. I truly believe that our reduced heating costs over the past couple of years can probably be correlated with Hub's use of tape.

There isn't a single day that passes when that child doesn't use tape. I know I should probably be annoyed by the massive use of tape. I know most people don't like things taped to their walls, doors, and floors. But, in all honesty, I find it adorable. Each time Hub uses tape, I know he is using his imagination and/or his problem-solving skills. Both of those are really important things, and I feel like they are far more valuable than the time I spend peeling tape off the house and everything in it. Every time I hear that screech of tape being unrolled, I know Hub is up to something, and I'm just grateful it is something worthwhile.

Day 17: What are you thankful for today?

Day 18: Today I am thankful for liquid soap.

For many years, soap and I have had our differences. It began as a child. Those grimy soap bars covered in dirt and suds made me cringe. Reaching out to lather up after a good stint outdoors, I could feel myself spreading cooties. I was soundly convinced it was me who had started the cooties epidemic, and I knew that behind their usually clean appearance that those soapy fiends called soap bars were the masterminds behind its spread. I needed a way out of the evil scheme. Liquid soap was my answer. Somehow, pumping that little white pump with the side of my dirty hand made me feel immensely better about my role in the whole cooties scandal. As a result, I was able to at long last become a card-carrying member of the Anti-Cooties League, those admirable girls who didn't have cooties to spread.

Years later, soap and I butted heads again. I had always had super-sensitive skin, and there was only one kind of soap bar I could use. Although the major brands had lured me into trying them by their claims of being hypoallergenic or safe for sensitive skin, they all turned out to be too strong. Unfortunately, the one soap bar I could use must not have been a popular soap, and it became harder and harder to find. It felt as if soap were trying to get even with me. After all, I had turned my back on the dreaded soap bar, and I knew the soap bar initiative had never really forgiven me for taking action to stop the cooties epidemic. I was scared that I was doomed to a life of itching skin and red spots. Again, liquid soap came to the rescue. It was then that I came to the realization that liquid soap and I were meant for great things.

More years have passed, and soap and I have yet to make amends. Liquid soap has remained my trusted pal, seeing me through many years of cootie-free living. These days, that bond has been strengthened by my children's sensitive skin. They, too, cannot tolerate the dreaded soap bar, and liquid soap has assumed leadership of our tiny household dirt brigade. Through mud wars and cake fights, smashed prunes and Vaseline hair gel experiments, liquid soap has managed to get the job done. So today I am thankful for liquid soap, a little blessing that has had a big impact on my life. Thanks, liquid soap! Here's to another 60 years of camaraderie!

Day 18: What are you thankful for today?

Day 19: Today I am thankful for forgiveness.

Forgiveness is an amazing thing, but it often brings up strong emotions when broached in conversation. Some people may react with joy and gratefulness, while others may react with anger and condemnation. I know those emotions may cover an entire realm of topics, but rarely can one subject create such polar emotions. Even more perplexing is the thought process behind each and the ties both situations hold.

I'm lucky enough to live in the Bible belt, and around here we may as well be the buckle on that belt. So when people bring up the subject of forgiveness, we usually associate it with Jesus. We do this because we are so grateful for Christ's sacrifice for us, an immeasurable gift that granted us salvation. I know personally that I can't express my gratitude for such a gift. Through Christ we are forgiven for our sins, without judgment or reprisal, and therefore we often feel strong emotions like love and thankfulness when forgiveness comes up. Why wouldn't we be happy? Christ's love for us is unconditional, and asking is all it takes for forgiveness to be granted. Unfortunately, when it comes to our lives, this isn't always the case.

It seems that, in my experience, the other occasion when forgiveness comes up is when people don't want to talk about it. Usually this is when discussing the personal act of forgiving someone who has somehow wronged us. In these cases, forgiveness is often greeted without a very open mind. In fact, I have heard hundreds of times in my life that certain acts aren't forgivable or that a person doesn't deserve to be forgiven. It took me a while to see things differently, possibly because those very ideas about granting forgiveness were the most common reaction I heard for most of my life. Even working with therapists, this seemed to be a popular notion. Even then I challenged it.

So, some things aren't forgivable. Really? Why not? When Christ forgives us of our sins, is he in any way saying that suddenly the bad things we did are now okay? Does his forgiveness of a murderer suddenly erase the murder? No. Forgiveness has nothing to do with justification. Christ's forgiveness of our sins is not a change in moral stance. It is a clean slate for the future. With people, it is the same thing.

This is where many people get angry and stop listening. But this is a crucial point. When we grant people forgiveness, we are in no way saying that WHAT the person did is okay. What we are saying is that said act is no longer our concern. It doesn't mean that the person who committed the act is right or that the act is right. In the end, it just says that we aren't going to let said act effect our actions and emotions any longer. Some may say this is a strange position, but it all goes back to the idea that we shouldn't let people or emotions live rent-free in our heads. Forgiveness is as much a personal gift for us as it is a gift to the person to whom we grant it.

Still, people will argue that a person doesn't deserve forgiveness. Jesus didn't decide to forgive me because I earned it or deserved it. I never could. In fact, if Jesus were to wait to grant me forgiveness until I deserved it, I would never receive it. If we're honest, none of us would. I don't know a single person alive today who didn't at some point in time sin. If we were sinless, we wouldn't need to be forgiven. Christ's sacrifice wouldn't have been necessary. We could have made our way to Heaven on our own.

It's the same when it comes to us forgiving other people. If we wait around until someone deserves our forgiveness, we will most likely never have to grant it. There are some people who will never change or feel bad about a decision they have made. There are also people who may feel bad and try to change but fail. Oftentimes, holding on to anger and hurt in the end hurts us more than the person who committed the act. Forgiveness allows us to say that the act—no matter how wrong or bad—no longer has a hold on us. Our granting forgiveness frees us more than it frees the person who wronged us.

I know that no one—not even me—can grant forgiveness as readily as Christ. I don't expect to, nor do I expect anyone else to. I just know that, in my life, forgiveness was the first step in so many steps towards living a more peaceful, satisfying life. Forgiving didn't mean I had forgotten what happened or that I thought what happened was right or justified. It simply meant that I had finally reached a point where I understood I was the one being hurt by not forgiving. It meant I had reached a point where moving forward meant letting go of the past. And it meant I finally had decided to follow in Christ's footsteps. He forgave me, a sinner with a list of sins a mile long who is still struggling with sin, without waiting for me to be worthy. His forgiveness was a gift to me, granting me a place in Heaven with a brother and two grandmothers I love. I am thankful I can pass that gift on to others. I hope you might, too.

Day 19: What are you thankful for today?

Day 20: Today I am thankful for commas.

When I was in elementary school, commas seemed pretty simple. You used a comma to join two complete sentences, and you used a comma to separate items in a list. It seemed like commas were not all that complicated. By the time I went to high school, commas had a few more duties. You used a comma after or before someone's name when you addressed them, and you used a comma in place of a period in a quotation when you were adding an identifier to designate who was speaking. Commas were getting a little more complicated, but they were still within my grasp. Once high school came along, however, commas had more duties than I ever expected. I wasn't sure if I could master them, but I knew I was going to give it my best.

I set out on my comma mission with full force. I memorized and memorized. I practiced and practiced. I tried, despite friend after friend's surrender to the perplexity of commas, to win the uphill battle with those periods with tails. I diagramed sentence upon sentence. I dissected clause after clause. I sought commas out, challenging them to beat me. Many a time, I thought I was a goner. It seemed that, no matter how much I memorized, I was never going to conquer the comma. I grew a bit bitter at using them. So as I waved goodbye to high school, I waved my white surrender flag to the comma.

Off to college I went, but that dreadful comma followed me. Even worse, he followed me in two additional languages. My love of words prompted me to minor in French and study abroad in Russia. Unfortunately, as French and Russian get harder, so does the use of commas—just like in English. War had been declared again, and this time I would not lose. I tried and tried, and, after many years and different schools, I had all but defeated the comma. I could use it here, and I could use it there. I could use them everywhere! Yet, there was just one thing missing. I couldn't name it or put my finger on it, but something was missing.

Two years ago, I finally discovered what had been missing. I began editing college papers to help pay the bills. I gained a regular client named Jane, a graduate student from Korea, who spoke English as a second language. She had a very difficult time writing her papers in formal English, and I was experienced in both English grammar and her field of study, counseling. It seemed to be a perfect match. As one paper turned into ten, I began to notice something strange. Jane could mix up any sentence, rearranging the subject and verb or confusing one word for another. Many times, it felt more like interpreting than editing. Yet Jane could find the right place for the majority of her commas.

As I read sentence after sentence aloud, trying to understand it, I finally realized something I had never understood before. Reading those mixed and mashed sentences with the correctly placed commas, I finally could hear the place when I took a breath. I had never actually heard it before. At least never that clearly. A light bulb went off in my head. It felt like I could actually see the light bulb glowing it was so huge. Suddenly, all of those years of studying and practicing made sense. *Commas help a reader know when to take a breath.* It had been told to me over and over, but, with my speedy Southern woman speech, it had always been too difficult to hear. Reading the English of someone who only spoke English as a second language made me realize just how much control the writer does have over the reader. A writer even gets to tell a reader when to breathe. I don't know how much more control a writer could want, but, it seems to me, that such a huge amount of control should be used very wisely.

These days, commas are one of my favorite things. Working as an editor, I see them all the time. There are a few people who throw in a few too many, but, in most cases, the majority of people don't use nearly enough. As I plow through papers and short stories, I read them aloud in my head, adding that pause to breathe for commas. I even say the word commas as I add them, perhaps hoping it will make them magically appear. It is a very difficult process to describe, but it works. By adding in that little word *comma* wherever a comma is needed helps me actually hear the pause. If I ever have a doubt, I add in the word to my reading. Doing this helps my brain actually process the pause when my Southern-induced-speech-speed gets in the way. The more I get to know the comma, the better I like it. To me, using a comma is a privilege not to be taken lightly or haphazardly, and I now strive to give the comma its due. I have found that my understanding of those tricky, little, long-tailed breath markers is not as common a thing as I would have thought. This understanding gives me an ability to do work many people would not enjoy, correcting grammar day after day. I am thankful for this magnificent blessing. My hope is to help others find their peace with commas, one editing job at a time.

Day 20: What are you thankful for today?

Day 21: Today I am thankful for rainy days.

Rainy days are possibly my favorite kind of days. I love them. I know most people associate rainy days with feeling sad or blue, but they seem to make me genuinely happy. There is something magical about rainy days—some innate allure that sunny days just don't have. Rainy days come in all shapes and sizes, and, in all honesty, it's hard for me to decide which kind I love the best. There are hot ones, cold ones, fierce ones, and calm ones. Each one holds its own special charm, making the decision absolutely impossible.

Summer rainy days hold the possibility of puddles and dances. A nice warm rain on a nice warm day is the perfect weather for a walk. Summer shoes make puddles all the more fun, letting the water run through your toes and the mud squish with each step. And, of course, there is the summer drizzle. That light misty rain just strong enough to dampen your hair, leaving tiny water-droplet condensation on each strand. Women often complain of getting the frizzies when it rains, but I say it just helps bring out my natural curl. There is just something adorable about those fly-away hairs parading this way and that. I love it. Those misty, grey days are also perfect for a dance in the grass—twirling, whirling, and looking for rainbows. What more could a girl ask for?

Cold rainy days may even be better than hot ones. Cold rainy days are the perfect pajama days. Oh what comfort, walking around all day in your pajamas! Even better is curling up under a thick blanket next to a window, the curtains pulled back to let in that dim white light from the sun hidden behind clouds. Add a book and a cup of steaming, hot tea and it's bliss. Rainy days just magnify the coziness and security of being at home.

Even on wintery rainy days out and about, it is calming to listen to the rhythm of the swooshing windshield wipers, beating out the pace of the rain. People take on such a romantic quality on days like that: rushing in and out, dancing around puddles, dashing for doors. It's like watching a real-life romance movie in action. I always half-expect to see lovers embracing inside doorways and to hear the rise of theatrical music. Sometimes, when I try hard enough, I do.

Even stormy rainy days are amazing. The giant claps of thunder, applauding the miracle that is rain, and the beautiful crackles of lightning splitting the sky. It's beauty in motion, a giant symphony. Rain storms all start, play out, and finish differently, and they do so in ways man-made music could never accomplish. Thunder and lightning make up the percussion section of the orchestra, while the wind plays the woodwinds and the rain plays the strings. They move together, slow then fast. Loud then soft. Thousands of fingers plucking harp strings as raindrops fall. The strong wind's bassoon followed by the crash of thunder's cymbals. Taking time to enjoy that music makes storms a little less scary and a little more amazing.

Calm rainy days bring peace and tranquility. The pitter patter of raindrops on rooftops soothes the soul, God's tears to make things clean and new. The ashen sky serves as a giant, cotton ball muffler for the world, and life becomes quiet. There is a certain stillness to the world rarely found in these busy times. Poets can write the sweetest lines on days like these for hearts can breathe when there is a hush on the world.

There have been many rainy days in my lifetime, each of them different. The rainy days made by nature, however, always seem to be the best. The next time a rainy day comes along, take time to enjoy it. The Lord fills each of them with their own gifts, and if you listen long enough, you can find them.

Day 21: What are you thankful for today?

Day 22: Today I am thankful for deadlines.

Deadlines. Those impending markers of doom. They are dreaded, detested, and feared. There are few people I have ever met who actually enjoy deadlines. There was a time when I dreaded, detested, and feared them myself. Fortunately, I can now count myself in the tremendously smaller group of people who don't mind them. In fact, I actually enjoy them. All it took was a change of mind to create this change of heart. Here's my secret.

I have always held firm to the belief that a job well done is reward enough in itself. I don't need money or a prize to complete a task. My parents thought doing things for ourselves was the best way for us to become self-motivated individuals. I totally agree with them. I didn't receive money for good grades, despite year upon year of honor roll certificates. I wasn't given incentives to perform jobs or complete tasks. I saw them as part of life. So, even now, I have a hard time saying that you should give yourself a prize because you completed a task.

At the same time, I am a chronic procrastinator. Being a procrastinator makes life much less fun and much more complicated. I also habitually underestimate the amount of time I will need to successfully complete a task. Combine both of these factors with my refusal to give myself a reward for finishing on time, and, to many people, this looks like a completely hopeless situation. Looking at it on paper, it almost feels like it should be. But it's not.

I have discovered that deadlines are actually beneficial. This discovery took into account my inability to plan enough time for something to be completed, my refusal to "pay" myself to complete a task, and my tendency to wait to the last minute. Instead of using deadlines to tell me when I have to get something finished , I use them to tell myself when something else is about to start. Sounds kind of like a reward, doesn't it? Not really.

For example, say I have a big project due on Friday evening. On Sunday of that week, I sit down and look at my calendar. I look ahead at what events are coming up or what I have been hoping to accomplish. Let's say I have been really looking forward to spending an evening with the kids playing and just spending time with them. (This type of activity works well for me because I love spending time with my kids and like to schedule in play time.) I simply plan play time for Friday night. Here is where the difference between reward and motivation comes in. The paper is due Friday night. In the past, that would mean me sitting on the computer all night long trying to type a paper into the computer a mile a minute and having to ignore everything I love doing. I just scheduled my favorite thing to do at the same time. I ask myself, which do I choose? Of course, I choose the kids and playing. So that leaves me no choice but to finish the paper ahead of time so that I can get to do what I really want to do. It's not a reward for finishing; it's a motivation to finish.

This type of thing can apply to just about any type of situation. I use it with project deadlines all the time. I no longer think of the deadline as a deadline. Instead, it is a chance for me to get to do something I enjoy. In a round-about way it may be a reward, but in my thinking it is a motivation. I have also found that thinking of the deadline as something to finish before I get to the fun thing I want to do helps me to not worry so much about the deadline. It has been clinically proven that anticipation of a positive event can raise mood levels and elevate the chemical levels of multiple neurotransmitters in the brain that make us happy. Positive anticipation is a much better feeling than worry or dread. I am excited about my plans and often forget to worry about the project I am working on. I see the project as one more thing to finish instead of a single entity that is weighing me down and making me feel crazy. So it takes tension and nervousness and turns it into adrenaline and serotonin and makes me feel better.

So, if you take a bad deadline and make it into a good event that replaces it (but you have to keep in mind that you can't go if you don't finish it, kind of like the steps in a project or recipe—you can't leave out a step) you ease worry and re-focus on a different aspect of positive thinking. I think this could work for just about any deadline or project you finish. For example, I have to work on this book project before I get to work on my crafts. Even on days when nothing comes, I still try to write at least a little so I will be able to say I worked on it and get to do something I would like to do. It's worth a try, and you may even find you, too, will love deadlines.

Day 22: What are you thankful for today?

Day 23: Today I am thankful for pipe tobacco.

Smells can so easily trigger memories. It's almost as if there is a direct link from our noses to the part of our brain that stores memories, and, even though I am sure there are scientific studies about whether or not such a correlation exists, I don't need science to tell me it really works. The smell of cinnamon and apples reminds me of my mom's kitchen, and the smell of cut grass reminds me of hot, summer days in the South. Cocoa butter smells like the beach, and evergreen trees smell like Christmas. Johnson's baby wash smells like my kids, and my favorite lotion smells like a birthday cake baking. My husband's old flannel shirt I wore for years smells like him, a warm, musky smell that still makes me feel safe and loved. Smell is such an essential part of my memories, yet I am always surprised at how readily they can conjure up the person, place, or time I associate with them.

My older brother had several items over his life that he loved more than others. He loved Mountain Dew and Cheerwine. He loved whales. And when we were very young, he loved the smell of Borkum Riff pipe tobacco. I am not sure where he developed his love of that certain tobacco or how many years he loved it, but it seemed like he carried a canister or pouch of it with him for ages. My brother was severely disabled, and I suppose his attachment to certain things may have been related to his disability, but it may have just been who he was. Either way, I smelled that sweet, aromatic tobacco day in and day out as a young child. He carried a canister of that tobacco like some kids carry a blanket or stuffed animal, and, looking back, I can't help but wonder if maybe the smell made him think of something that he made him feel warm and safe. I will probably never know for sure why he loved it so much. I just know he did.

Time passed, and my brother's attachment moved on to whales and soda. Borkum Riff became another memory, buried in some file folder in the back of my brain. Every so often, however, something magical happens. I may be in the middle of a store or walking across a parking lot to get to my car, but that heady smell of pipe tobacco finds its way to my nose. Somehow, I always stop in my tracks and take a deep breath. My eyes close, even if only for a moment, and I am transported back to those days of my childhood. My brother stands before me laughing and smiling that happy, giant smile that closed his eyes it shone so brightly, and I can almost reach out and hug him. He seems so close, even though it's been over four years since I had such a chance. Surprisingly, I don't end up at those times like I am right now, crying and sniffing. I end up smiling. For a single moment in time I can see and hear my brother as if he were still here with me, and it's glorious.

I don't know how smells do it. I don't know if I want to know how they do it. I just know they do. I also know I could readily buy a package of that old pipe tobacco, but it wouldn't have the magic of those stolen moments that happen by on a passing breeze. So, as a brisk wind blows past me on this chilly November night, I will lift my nose with anticipation. There's no telling what memories might blow my way. That little whiff of Borkum Riff pipe tobacco may be just around the bend.

Day 23: What are you thankful for today?

Day 24: Today I am thankful to have a King.

I have tried to find things during this collection that anyone could encounter or might have in their possession. I have searched high and low for items I have a sentimental connection to or that may just be something that was particularly useful that day. And, although I am thankful every day for this blessing, I feel no collection of thankfulness would be complete without being thankful for my King. I happen to have a King that many others have, and, no, it is definitely not Elvis. It is Jesus Christ.

I started my religious journey at the age of seven when I was saved in a Baptist church where a preacher preached hellfire and damnation. Along the road, I attended Church of God churches with women speaking tongues and people waving arms and fainting. I visited Independent Baptist churches, Southern Baptist churches, and non-denominational churches. I went to mass at a Catholic church or two, and I even entertained the notion of practicing Buddhism. Many years and many detours later, I arrived at a little Episcopal church named St. Michael's and finally found my home.

My kids were still little when we first visited St. Michael's. Diddle was still super afraid of strangers, so our search for a church was often cut short by her bursting into tears and screaming in terror as we walked through the church doors. That particular summer morning, we braced ourselves as we approached the glass front doors of the little church. As we opened the door, the current rector, Father Workman, stood before us in the reception area. Diddle ran inside and went straight up to him. Patrick and I were blown away. It may have helped that Father Workman looked a good bit like Santa Claus, the white hair and beard and a certain jovial look in his merry eyes. I think, though, that she just felt safe and welcome there, and we knew St. Michael's was where we would stay.

A few months later, the children and I were baptized, something I had only really thought of since we started attending St. Michael's. Scared that water being poured over her head might frighten Diddle, Father Workman had planned to anoint her head with water. After seeing me have water poured over my head, Diddle walked right up and bent her head to have water poured over hers, as well. Even little Hub did wonderfully. St. Michael's truly started my family's spiritual journey together, and for that I am forever grateful. We still attend, although we have let life get in the way more times than we would like, and, even though we are now ministered to by a new rector, Father Lee, we are still learning and growing along the way.

Last winter, I reached a very low time in my life. Even though I had been on my personal spiritual journey for over thirty years, the Lord wasn't quite finished working on me. I had been out of work for almost a year, unable to find even a job waiting tables due to my poor health and inability to do as much physically as most jobs require these days. Money was low, and of course that makes everything seem worse. I had bought a giant bag of books for three dollars at a local thrift store and filled it with over a hundred books, planning to sell them in a yard sale and make a profit by selling them at ten cents apiece. Little did I know why I had truly bought those books.

Among those book were several religious books, and, after sorting through them, I picked up one on hopeless situations. It was a tiny book, maybe twenty pages long, with a painting of a man on the cover with long grey hair and tears in his eyes. I had no idea why I was drawn to it, except I felt like my own life was a hopeless situation. I took it in the bathroom with me for some quiet time where the children were less likely to disturb me while I read it, which seems even odder to me now since I never read in the bathroom. I felt like every word had been written for me. I felt like the Lord had sent it to me on purpose, and I broke down in tears, praying my heart out to the Lord to take over my life and guide me. I left that room feeling better.

Since that day, things have been up and down in my life. Money is still beyond tight. We are absolutely broke based on what little money we have. Amazingly enough, I don't mind. Now, I openly admit that I hate not being financially secure, and I am beyond grateful for our family that helps and supports us and all that the Lord has provided for us. The reason I don't mind so much about our lack of money is that I know in my heart that our bank account in Heaven is overflowing. I have been able to teach my children about the Lord and be part of their schoolwork. My husband and I can pray together, and we can share Bible stories with our kids. Every day I see ways that the things that have happened this past year have strengthened our family in the Lord, and I have no words to express my gratitude for it.

I know I should have been able to do those things before, pray with my husband and teach my kids. I did. The thing is that now I yearn to do those things. I feel driven to know more about the Lord and to have the Lord play a part in our everyday lives. He has given us so much. It means so much to me to know that I can pass this yearning on to my children. Every day when I see them stop and pray, I know I am doing my job. This past Sunday at church, my children gave a dollar apiece to the church's offering collection. The tradition at our church is that each offering is accompanied by the sharing of what the contributor is thankful for that day. These are called Thank Offerings, and all the offerings go to local charities. My daughter was thankful that we were able to be at church, something I was thankful for, too. My son was thankful that Jesus is his King, something that inspired this entry. Not a day goes by when I am not thankful for that very thing, and today I wanted to share that thankfulness with you.

I don't know your heart. There is no way I possibly could. But I know mine. I know I love the Lord and am thankful that Jesus is my King. I also know that every day since I made that decision has not been any less taxing on my body or my mind. Being a Christian isn't a cure for things like work or bills. But I know it has been less taxing on my heart. I am thankful I can share this love of the Lord with you, and I hope if you don't know Him that you may look at the words I write in this book and consider finding out more about Him. I know how thankful I am to have Jesus as my Savior and King. He is ready to be yours, too.

Day 24: What are you thankful for today?

Day 25: Today I am thankful for technology.

This morning my husband went to the auto store to buy a part to fix his car. The car has been acting strange for a week or more, and, after consulting with his trusted, local mechanic, Patrick made the decision to try and fix the car on his own. The treatment for the car's diagnosis was to replace a spark plug, and, with the help of do-it-yourself videos on YouTube, Patrick felt prepared for the job. *Score one for technology because seeing someone actually find the correct bolt to unscrew and the correct way to remove the plugs is a whole lot easier for a beginner than using a manual with hand-drawn pictures that may or may not look at all like what's underneath the hood of your car.*

When my husband arrived at the auto store, he obtained the correct part and went to the register to pay. The cashier rang up the items and asked for payment. My husband produced his debit card. The cashier slid the card and made an unpleasant face, turning and informing my husband that the card had been denied. Completely befuddled, my husband asked the clerk to repeat the procedure only to have the same end result. Patrick had checked the bank account before leaving home to see that all the bills were up-to-date, and there had been plenty of money then. He pulled out his cell phone and called the bank. According to the automated system, there was plenty of money in the account. Patrick then used his cell phone to call me so that I would not try to use my card somewhere until he found out what was going on with the account. *Score two, three, and four for technology: automated customer service, online banking, and cell phones.*

At the bank, my husband discovered that someone had tried to use his bank card number that morning for a $109 purchase at a store in Florida—not even our own state! The bank was able to place a hold on our account so that the fraudulent activity could be stopped. *Score five for technology.* Although it may seem somewhat frightening how the bank system could detect the fraudulent activity, discovering someone using your card number illegally immediately after it happened was a *whole* lot easier on us than finding out when all of our money was gone. What ended up being a thirty-minute hassle could have been much worse. It could have meant no money to pay for water or power. It could have meant no mortgage payment or no gas to go to work. One little alert saved us so much heartache and headache. We are truly blessed.

I don't know if technology always wins the battle or if it is always the best thing. I do know that I am grateful to still have money in my account for power and food to keep my children fed and warm. I know some people would say technology caused the problem since it is technology that has allowed people to find out our bank numbers and such. In all fairness, I would usually agree. Among my friends and family, I openly admit that I remain one of the slowest to adapt to the changing times. I don't have a smartphone or satellite or cable TV. I don't have my computer on all day and night, and I try not to stay online any more than necessary. I just don't feel comfortable with computers running my life. Today, however, I am thankful technology was on our side. Everything has its purpose, and today I am grateful that technology did its job.

Day 25: What are you thankful for today?

Day 26: Today I am thankful for ties.

When ties come to mind, most people probably think about Father's Day or church or weddings. For a mom on a tight budget, however, ties are a versatile, inexpensive opportunity to get crafty. Some people call this trend to reuse as up-cycling. I choose to call it making something incredibly neat that is also extraordinarily fun and affordable and the answer to my prayers.

When Christmas rolled around this year, we were on a very tight budget. We have been on a tight budget for a while now, but this Christmas seemed to be tighter then we had hoped. I went to the Lord in prayer, asking him to help us find a way to afford gifts for all the gifts we needed to give. He answered by introducing me to the many crafty gifts that can be made from a simple necktie. Necklaces, cases for eyeglasses, cozies, cell phone cases, bracelets, and purse straps are all possibilities. Ties can be made into dozens of attractive, trendy gifts at a price that won't break the bank. Some can be found for as little as one dollar per tie in consignment or thrift shops. With a little bit of love and creativity, they can be transformed into great gifts. And so, I am beyond grateful that I found a fun, creative way to make so many great presents, each unique and made with a lot of love.

My tie creations could be easily made by anyone with a basic knowledge of sewing, a few ideas from photos online, a bag of second-hand ties, and a needle and thread. I first ran across a picture of a necktie necklace on Pinterest, the site every girl who ever wanted to be crafty but never was has fallen in love with, me included. I usually used it to find out more about a certain project I had planned rather than to find new ideas. When I ran across the necktie necklace, I just knew the Lord had led me to the right place. I thanked the Lord, and then I got to work.

I found a great website that had a photo of one and some simple directions. The next day I found some affordable ties at our local thrift store, and I came home to get to work. I folded, pressed, and stitched the most adorable necklace. It looked really neat—not quite what I had seen on the internet, but it sure was striking. I went on to make necklaces for two present-swaps with family for Christmas. I also designed hair bands for my little girl, soda can cozies, and several attractive cell phone cases. Even better, it has been a ton of fun.

Ties may seem like an unusual thing to be thankful for, but I am. I am thankful the Lord answered my prayers, for the presents these ties have made, and the fun I have had and will have using them for craft ideas. It's amazing how something that simple and ordinary can make such a huge difference in life. A week ago, I would have had no idea a tie could have so much meaning for me. I also had no clue how I was going to come up with creative, attractive gifts for Christmas. I went to the Lord in prayer, asking him to help me be able to find a way to afford gifts for the holidays. He did. He led me to these awesome homemade crafts. It just goes to show that the Lord works in mysterious ways and is present even in the simplest things.

Day 26: What are you thankful for today?

Day 27: Today I am thankful for creditors.

My sweet six-year-old son is always running on overdrive, ninety miles a minute. He often has a difficult time understanding people, although he has had his hearing professionally tested and everything is fine. I truly think he just listens better at some times than others. The result is that some words do not come in or out as clearly as they might should. Today the result also left me extraordinarily happy to hear a new take on a word that usually fills my heart with a sense of dread.

We were driving down the road to the doctor's office, and Hub and Diddle had been singing along to the radio. A commercial had come on, and so the kids began to talk. Hub and Diddle chatted a little about one thing or another in nature, the life cycle and feeding habits of this and that. Hub then had an announcement he was certain he wanted me to hear, as well.

"Mommy, did you know that even rattlesnakes have creditors?"

"Huh?" I said as I looked at him through the rearview mirror.

"Even rattlesnakes have creditors," Hubby repeated.

Here, I honestly laughed. In my mind, I could see a rattlesnake huddling in a corner, begging a giant man in a suit to just give him another month to come up with the money. I could see that snake, a creature that usually strikes fear in my own heart, slinking away, filled with a dread and fear I knew myself. Maybe my own experiences were blinding me, but I thought it was the funniest thing I had ever heard.

"King snakes are creditors of rattlesnakes," Hub continued, obviously thinking my laughter was because I thought he was incorrect.

At this point, the giant businessman towering over the rattlesnake, whose tail was now rattling fiercely, was a king snake in full regalia with gold crown towering on its head. I sucked in my laughter, and attempted to answer little Hub.

"I think you mean predator, Hub."

"Yeah, I know. I said 'predator.'"

"Okay," I answered, feeling better that I had helped repair his pride.

It was the sweetest mistake I could imagine, but man was it a great laugh for me on a day that could have been considered a pretty lousy one. Nothing beats a rattlesnake creditor on a rough day.

Day 27: What are you thankful for today?

Day 28: I am thankful for groceries.

Carrying in arm after arm of groceries, I could complain about how heavy they are or how poorly they were packed. I could gripe about the rising prices and the house down-payment it takes to feed a family of four for a week. I could whine about the twenty-minute trip home from the store or the bumper-to-bumper traffic. Or I could be thankful I have them. Not everyone is so lucky.

This year has been a rough one for our family financially, but, then again, it has been a rough one for millions of others as well. Each month when the bills come in and the money goes out, we seem to be left with less and less. So many I know have also felt the tightening of purse strings. In a country supposedly recovering from a recession, many families seem to be stuck in a depression. At the end of the day, there will be Americans from every walk of life going to bed hungry.

Every week I head to the grocery store, armed with coupons and lists compiled after searching the sales advertisements and taking careful inventory at home. Sugar, milk, eggs, butter, bread—items many take for granted week in and week out. The list never seems to get shorter, and the prices only seem to go up. But, as I pass by other shoppers, I see so clearly the end result. Buggies that once were piled full are barely halfway up. Babies riding in the buggy seat can no longer reach the groceries loaded in the back. Even more obvious is the smaller number of groceries on the store shelves. Cans that were once stacked to the back of the shelf now line the edge, leaving empty holes when one is removed.

It's awful to me that something once considered a necessity is beginning to be seen as a luxury. I watch the news and read online about arguments to cut Food Stamps, forcing people in need to buy less food and spend more wisely. If you've never been unfortunate enough to live off the groceries Food Stamps provide, I urge you try to feed a family of four on $380 a month. It's not as easy as it sounds considering four gallons of milk and four loaves of bread cost between thirty and forty dollars. Often the poorest people know more about conservation and budgeting than the economists and politicians would have you think.

Still, there is a huge need in this country for help for so many families. There is a reason why everywhere you turn there are pleas for food for children going home to no food all weekend long, food for empty food banks, and food for homeless shelters. People in America are starving, and not all of them are there by choice nor are all of them drug users or criminals. Jobs are lost, workplaces aren't hiring as much, and when there are hundreds of people seeking out the same single opening for a minimum wage job not everyone gets hired. I completely understand that a few people can spoil it for the rest of the people, but is the food that sustains life really a place where we should let that misconception be our reasoning?

Today I urge you to open your cabinets and take inventory. Do you have three boxes of noodles and only need two? Did you take advantage of that sale last week and buy ten cans of soup for $10, knowing you only plan to eat three this week and next? Is there a box of cake mix you don't need that could be used to bake a birthday cake for some child in poverty? If there is, then look into your heart and ask yourself what you would hope others would do if you had nothing and their cabinets held extra. There is goodness in the world, and we can all choose to be a part of it. Today I choose to be thankful, and I choose to be giving. What do you choose?

Thank you, Lord, for this food we have. Not everyone I know has this much. Not everyone I know can even dream this. I am beyond blessed to have food to eat not only on my table but in my cabinets, as well. I can't help but feel humbled when I think of those who have nothing. I pray that I may help at least one person to feel thankful today who wasn't, even if that person turns out to be me. No matter how little we have, there is always someone who has less. I am thankful for this day and this food.

Day 28: What are you thankful for today?

Day 29: I am thankful for crayons.

During elementary school, crayons were my best friends. My art teacher, Mrs. Sullivan, thrilled me each week with some amazing lesson on color, technique, or creativity. I even joined an afterschool program my fifth grade year based on my artistic abilities. The art world lay before me.

When I began middle school at age eleven, I laid down my paint brushes and pencils, planning to pick them up a little later on. The torment of middle school seemed bad enough without adding artsy to the long list of derogatory descriptors with which my peers were not afraid to chide me (others included nerd, too-tall, freckle face, and so on).

The dread of middle school soon turned into the low self-esteem of high school, and, by this point, I had begun to doubt whether or not I ever did have any artistic talent. Looking at the requirements for art classes and the caliber of work I had to stand up against, I knew I would fail. Given that such a failure would only drive my self-esteem lower, I decided to postpone art again and pick it up in my spare time. Since spare time was in short supply, art remained at the bottom of my to-do list.

Days turned into months, and months turned into years. So much time had passed that I came to wonder if I would ever pick art up again. I reached the age of 30, and I still had not returned to art. I actually forgot that I had even a drop of artistic talent. It wasn't until I began teaching that I remembered I could draw a few basic pictures. Even so, I was too busy and unfocused to take the time to truly consider art as something I could do.

When my children finally took to drawing, I began to remember how fun drawing could be. Their little fingers gripped the brightly colored crayons, pushing and pulling colorful wax trails all over the page. They smiled so brightly when they made marks on the paper. Looking at their beaming faces, I realized how amazing being able to create was. I picked up a crayon and began to draw. Colors moved across the paper, and I felt genuinely happy. Something so simple brought joy to my heart.

Little honest words of encouragement flowed from my children's mouths to my heart. For the first time in decades, I was drawing my heart out. Day after day, we drew colored lines and squiggles. Coloring book after coloring book filled up, and my children's love of drawing grew as mine was rediscovered. Art became part of our lives.

Over the last few years, my children's creativity has grown by leaps and bounds, and I have rediscovered a part of me that desperately needed to be rediscovered. Art has added to my relationship with my children and even with my husband, who, without even a little prompting, has gotten out his paint brushes and shaken off the dust. We now have a wonderful activity to share with each other, and our support for each other's creativity has helped our love of art to grow.

Today I encourage you to look inside and see what creative outlet you might find. You may consider art, music, writing, knitting, sewing, sculpting, baking, model building, or carving. The list of activities is inexhaustible. I also encourage you to think of the people around you to see if there is someone who needs a little encouragement to pursue his talent. Creative outlets are so much more than a hobby. They are a way to find something beautiful inside of ourselves and to share encouragement and support with others. A few honest words can make the difference between a grey world and a world of color.

Day 29: What are you thankful for today?

Day 30: Today I am thankful for second chances.

Have you ever gotten a song stuck in your head? That one line that repeats over and over, everywhere you go, all day long? This month I haven't been able to shake a Veggie Tales song from the movie *Jonah*. "My God Is the God of Second Chances" has followed me day in and day out all month, a steady soundtrack to my dreams. Having sung this song since I first began writing this book, I knew that there was some meaning behind it all. When it came time to write this last day's entry, I knew it had to be about second chances. Every day before, I made some excuse, saying it had been covered in other entries or it wouldn't make sense. Today it made sense. It's my job to tell you that God gives second chances. I've had many second chances, but, luckily, with the Lord, fifth chances still count as second chances.

There are many ways that second chances have played a part in my thankfulness journey. This vow to spend thirty days being thankful was something that I attempted last year and truly wanted to do better at this year. Each day I have tried to think about my day and the things around me, trying to find something others might encounter in their daily lives and be familiar enough with to be able to relate to what I write. It was also an opportunity for me to try and be thankful for the little things in life and even some of the things that aren't so little. Writing these daily entries was my second chance at actually seeking out things in my life to be grateful for rather than rehashing the list I am thankful for daily. This year was my do-over. I have written my thirty entries, but, unlike last year, I am not drooping and drained. I feel refreshed and truly grateful. This year was a second chance I was glad to have, and I know taking the thirty-day challenge again was the best decision I could have made. My heart needed to search for things in my life to be thankful for, and I have found a plethora of them.

My faith in the Lord being renewed and my heart finding peace was also a second chance. God loved me despite my blindness. He loved me despite my determination to be in control and do things my way. He loved me enough to forgive me even when I didn't deserve it. Even as a baptized Christian thinking I was on the right track, I needed a second chance to live my life the way the Lord wanted me to live. He gave me the opportunity to look into my own heart and find my way back to him with his Love guiding the way. When my heart received that joy and love, I felt the peace that surpasses all understanding, and my heart filled with a hunger to know the Lord and learn more about how my life could be filled with joy and truth for all times. What a wonderful gift He gave me! A second chance to get my life straightened out.

When it comes to second chances, I can't help but also think of my father. I am thankful for my father. He chose to love me and my older brother when he didn't have to love us. He was our step-father, and he had no obligation to love us when he met my mother. Many men would not have taken the chance on becoming the step-father of a child as severely disabled as my older brother, but my dad did. He even adopted us, although changing our names had nothing to do with the fact that he had already become our dad. We were his second family, and he was ours. He gave us a second chance by becoming a father who actually cared about us. He gave us a second chance at a home and a family. I know we gave him the same second chance, but the risk may have been bigger for him. So, again, we have second chance after second chance.

A while back my father gave me a notebook he had written in, filling every page. On the last page, my dad wrote me a note to explain what the notebook was. My dad told me that the Lord had led him to take notes at the sermons he attended so he could give those notes to me. My dad said the notes were written with me in mind. For four years my dad took notes, Sunday morning and Sunday evening after Sunday morning and Sunday evening. I have no clue exactly how many pages the notebook is or how many sermons my dad took notes on, but I know the Lord guided him to do the right thing. I know this because even though I have had the notebook for a while, I picked it up at the beginning of the month and began to read it. Page after page contained sermons of how the Lord gives people second chances.

I know all of these events may seem separate and unrelated to some people, but to me they are a winding course that led me here. To a place where I can be thankful for what I have and have been blessed with. To a place filled with love and compassion. To a place where I can find peace. This has been a crazy journey, and many days I could have truly given up. I searched and searched for the right words and the right things for which to be thankful. I hope that in some small way my journey has helped you, too.

I am thankful I had a second chance to complete the thirty days of thankfulness challenge. My plan now is to daily find something for which to be thankful. I hope you will, too.

"But thanks be to God! For through what Christ has done, he has triumphed over us so that now wherever we go he uses us to tell others about the Lord and to spread the Gospel like a sweet perfume."
2 Corinthians 2:14, *The Living Bible*

Day 30: What are you thankful for today?

Epilogue

My thirty-day thankfulness journey truly impacted my life, both the failure to finish the first one and the successful finishing of the second. Now every night when my family gathers to pray, we share what we are thankful for from our days. My husband and I pray that this one simple addition to our days will help cultivate a lifetime of thankfulness in our children. In our eyes, it has already begun to work. Prayers of thankfulness have been shared for everything from lost teeth to found hope. With four people living four lives, it also helps us find out more about each other's daily lives and what it is that encourages each of us individually to keep going. Even more, it has added such a wonderful, caring, kindness to our lives.

I encourage you to make thankfulness a part of your daily life, and I encourage you to start today. It is always the right time to begin a journey that can change your life. It is always a good idea, and it is always worth it. I believe in you and know that you can do it. It doesn't have to be as involved as this book. It can be as simple as writing a word or two on your calendar each day. Something that simple can open a whole new view of life, and, if others see your thankfulness, they, too, may be inspired to start.

You've already started your journey by reading this book and taking this challenge. Now put the thankfulness challenge to work in your daily life. Pick up a pen and write down your thankful thoughts, grab a crayon and draw a picture about why you are thankful, or turn on the computer and start typing away. Let's cultivate a generation of thankfulness and restore the thankfulness to generations who may have forgotten how to be thankful daily. It's a project that is worth every minute of work. I know you'll find something along the way that will make your heart truly happy. What are you waiting for? Spread the joy of a thankful life today!

About the Author

April J. Durham is an avid reader, an experienced editor, a fun-loving teacher and tutor, and a really lucky wife and mom. She graduated summa cum laude with a BA in Criminal Sociology and a minor in French from Clemson University, as well as with an MA in Professional Mental Health Counseling with a subspecialty in Family and Marriage Therapy from Webster University. Durham also studied Russian and Russian Political History at the Polytechnical University in St. Petersburg, Russia, where she met her husband Patrick. She has worked for the last three years with her husband at the little freelance editing and book design company that bears their name, Durham Editing and E-books.

Durham lives in Liberty, South Carolina, with her husband, their two children, and a red-headed, freckle-faced dog named Koko. Her favorite authors include Christopher Golden, Nancy Holder, Ryan Henry, M. L. Katz, Pablo Neruda, and Mary Higgins Clark, Her writing has been permanently influenced by Raymond Carver's slice-of-life shorts, as well. She has two published books of poetry, *All the Wrong Places* and *One Last Drag*. Durham has also compiled, edited, and choreographed six anthologies of writers from around the world into bestselling collections, as well as edited, formatted, and collaborated on numerous bestselling books.

30619558R00068

Made in the USA
Charleston, SC
20 June 2014